SHAKESPEARE

THE TAMING
OF THE
SHREW

NOTES

COLES EDITORIAL BOARD

Bound to stay open

Publisher's Note

Otabind (Ota-bind). This book has been bound using the patented Otabind process. You can open this book at any page, gently run your finger down the spine, and the pages will lie flat.

ABOUT COLES NOTES

COLES NOTES have been an indispensible aid to students on five continents since 1948.

COLES NOTES are available for a wide range of individual literary works. Clear, concise explanations and insights are provided along with interesting interpretations and evaluations.

Proper use of COLES NOTES will allow the student to pay greater attention to lectures and spend less time taking notes. This will result in a broader understanding of the work being studied and will free the student for increased participation in discussions.

COLES NOTES are an invaluable aid for review and exam preparation as well as an invitation to explore different interpretive paths.

COLES NOTES are written by experts in their fields. It should be noted that any literary judgement expressed herein is just that – the judgement of one school of thought. Interpretations that diverge from, or totally disagree with any criticism may be equally valid.

COLES NOTES are designed to supplement the text and are not intended as a substitute for reading the text itself. Use of the NOTES will serve not only to clarify the work being studied, but should enhance the readers enjoyment of the topic.

ISBN 0-7740-3795-4

© COPYRIGHT 1998 AND PUBLISHED BY
COLES PUBLISHING COMPANY
TORONTO - CANADA
PRINTED IN CANADA

Manufactured by Webcom Limited
Cover finish: Webcom's Exclusive **DURACOAT**

CONTENTS

Page No.

WILLIAM SHAKESPEARE: LIFE AND WORKS

Biographical Sketch 1
Shakespeare's Writings 4
Shakespeare's England 7
The Elizabethan Theater 10
Shakespeare's Artistry.................................. 13

THE TAMING OF THE SHREW

Sources.. 16
The Problem of Authorship 19
The Framework Device................................. 21
Classical and Romance Elements 23
Elizabethan Attitudes Toward Marriage 26
Plot Summary... 28
Characters in the Play 30
Summaries and Commentaries by Act and Scene
    INDUCTION 1 32
    INDUCTION 2 35
    ACT I • SCENE 1 38
             SCENE 2 43
    ACT II • SCENE 1 47
    ACT III • SCENE 1 53
             SCENE 2 56
    ACT IV • SCENE 1 60
             SCENE 2 64
             SCENE 3 67
             SCENE 4 71
             SCENE 5 73
    ACT V • SCENE 1 75
             SCENE 2 78
Character Sketches 82
Setting.. 86
Image Patterns 87
Shakespeare's Handling of the Shrew Theme 92
The Taming of the Shrew as Farce 94

Other Shakespearean Farces 95
The Battle of the Sexes 97
Selected Criticisms 101
Review Questions and Answers 111
Bibliography 119

WILLIAM SHAKESPEARE
LIFE AND WORKS
Biographical Sketch

The Early Years

Despite the scholarship it has spawned, our knowledge of Shakespeare's life is sketchy, filled with more questions than answers, even after we prune away the misinformation accumulated over the years. He was baptized on April 26, 1564, in Holy Trinity Church, Stratford-on-Avon. As it was customary to baptize children a few days after birth, we conjecture that he was born on April 23. The monument erected in Stratford states that he died on April 23, 1616.

William was the third child of John Shakespeare, who came to Stratford from Snitterfield before 1532 as a "whyttawer" (tanner) and glover, and Mary Arden, daughter of a wealthy "gentleman of worship" from Wilmecote. They married around 1557. Since John Shakespeare owned one house on Greenhill Street and two on Henley Street, we cannot be certain where William was born, though the Henley Street shrine draws many tourists each year. William's two older sisters died in infancy, but three brothers and two other sisters survived at least into childhood.

Shakespeare's father was fairly well-to-do, dealing in farm products and wool, and owning considerable property in Stratford. After holding a series of minor municipal offices, he was elected alderman in 1565, high bailiff (roughly similar to the mayor of today) in 1568 and chief alderman in 1571. There are no records of young Will Shakespeare's education (though there are many unfounded legends), but he undoubtedly attended the town school. Ben Jonson's line about Shakespeare's having "small *Latine*, and lesse *Greeke*" refers not to his education, but to his lack of indebtedness to the classical writers and dramatists.

On November 27, 1582, a licence to marry was issued to "Willelmum Shaxpere *et* Annam Whateley *de* Temple Grafton." On the next day a marriage bond for "Willm Shagspere" and "Anne Hathwey of Stratford" was signed by Fulk Sandells and John Richardson, farmers of Stratford. This bond stated that there was no "lawful let or impediment by reason of any precontract, consanguinity, affinity, or by any other lawful means whatsoever." Thus, "William and Anne [were] to be married together with once asking of the banns of matrimony." The problem of Anne Whateley has led many researchers and some detractors to argue all kinds of improbabilities, such as the existence of two different Shakespeares and the forging of documents to conceal Shakespeare's true identity. The actual explanation seems to be simple: the clerk who made the marriage licence entry apparently copied the name "Whateley" from a preceding entry, as a glance at the full sheet suggests. (Incidentally, Nicholas Rowe in his biography of Shakespeare, published in 1709, well before the discovery of these marriage records, gave Anne's name as Hathaway.) The problems of marriage with Anne Hathaway — he was 18 and she was 26 — and of the bond have caused similar consternation. Why did these two marry when there was such a discrepancy of age? Why only one saying of the banns (rather than the usual three)? Why the emphasis on a possible legal impediment? The answer here is not simple or definite, but the birth of a daughter, Susanna, baptized at Holy Trinity on May 26, 1583, seems to explain the odd circumstances. It should be recognized, however, that an engagement to marry was considered legally binding in those days (we still have breach-of-promise suits today), and that premarital relations were not unusual or frowned upon when an engagement had taken place. The circumstances already mentioned, Shakespeare's ensuing activities and his will bequeathing to Anne "my second best bed with the furniture" have suggested to some that their marriage was not entirely happy. Their other children, the twins Hamnet and Judith, were christened on February 2, 1585.

Theatrical Life

Shakespeare's years before and immediately after the time of his marriage are not charted, but rumor has him as an apprentice to a master butcher, or as a country teacher or an actor with some provincial company. He is supposed to have run away from whatever he was doing for livelihood and to have gone to London, where he soon attached himself to some theatrical group. At this time there were only two professional houses established in the London environs, The Theatre (opened in 1576) and The Curtain (opened in 1577). His first connection with the theater was reputedly as holder of horses; that is, one of the stage crew, but a most inferior assignment. Thereafter, he became an actor (perhaps at this time he met Ben Jonson), a writer and a director. Such experience had its mark in the theatricality of his plays. We do know that he was established in London by 1592, when Robert Greene lamented in *A Groatsworth of Wit* (September, 1592) that professional actors had gained priority in the theater over university-trained writers like himself: "There is an upstart Crow, beautified with our feathers, that with his *Tygers hart wrapt in a Players hyde,* supposes he is as well able to bombast out a lanke verse as the best of you: and beeing an absolute *Iohannes fac totum* [Jack-of-all-trades], is in his owne conceit the onely Shake-scene in a countrey." An apology for Greene's ill-humored statement by Henry Chettle, the editor of the pamphlet, appeared around December 1592, in *Kind-Hart's Dream*.

Family Affairs

To return to the known details of his family life, Shakespeare's son, Hamnet, was buried at Stratford on August 11, 1596; his father was given a coat of arms on October 20, 1596; and he purchased New Place (a refurbished tourist attraction today) on May 4, 1597. The London playwright obviously had not severed connections with his birthplace, and he was reflecting his new affluence by being known as William Shakespeare of Stratford-upon-Avon, in the County of Warwick, Gentleman. His father was buried in Stratford on September 8, 1601, and his mother, on September 9, 1608. His daughter, Susanna, married Dr. John Hall on June 5, 1607, and they had a child named Elizabeth. His other daughter, Judith, married Thomas Quiney on February 10, 1616, without special licence, during Lent, and was, therefore, excommunicated. Shakespeare revised his will on March 25, 1616, and was buried on April 25, 1616 (according to the parish register).

3

Shakespeare's Writings

Order of Appearance

Dating of Shakespeare's early plays, while based on inconclusive evidence, has tended to hover around the early 1590s. Almost certainly, it is his chronicles of Henry the Sixth that Philip Henslowe, an important theatrical manager of the day, referred to in his diary as being performed during March-May, 1592. An allusion to these plays also occurs in Thomas Nashe's *Piers Penniless His Supplication to the Devil* (August, 1592).

The first published work to come from Shakespeare's hand was *Venus and Adonis* (1593), a long stanzaic poem, dedicated to Henry Wriothesley, Earl of Southampton. A year later, *The Rape of Lucrece* appeared, also dedicated to Southampton. Perhaps poetry was pursued during these years because the London theaters were closed as a result of a virulent siege of plague. The *Sonnets*, published in 1609, may owe something to Southampton, who had become Shakespeare's patron. Perhaps some were written as early as the first few years of the 1590s. They were mentioned (along with a number of plays) in 1598 by Francis Meres in his *Palladis Tamia*, and sonnets 138 and 144 were printed without authority by William Jaggard in *The Passionate Pilgrim* (1599).

There is a record of a performance of *A Comedy of Errors* at Gray's Inn (one of the law colleges) on December 28, 1594, and, during early 1595, Shakespeare was paid, along with the famous actors Richard Burbage and William Kempe, for performances before the queen by the Lord Chamberlain's Men, a theatrical company formed the year before. The company founded the Globe Theatre on the south side of the Thames in 1599 and became the King's Men when James ascended the throne. Records show frequent payments to the company through its general manager, John Heminge. From 1595 through 1614 there are numerous references to real estate transactions and other legal matters, to many performances and to various publications connected with Shakespeare.

Order of Publication

The first plays to be printed were *Titus Andronicus,* around February, 1594, and the garbled versions of *Henry VI,*

4

Parts II and III, in 1594. Thereafter, *Richard III* appeared in 1597 and 1598; *Richard II,* in 1597 and twice in 1598; *Romeo and Juliet,* in 1597 (a pirated edition) and 1599, and many others. Some of the plays appear in individual editions, with or without Shakespeare's name on the title page, but 18 are known only from their appearance in the first collected volume (the so-called First Folio) of 1623. The editors were Heminge and Henry Condell, another member of Shakespeare's company. *Pericles* was omitted from the First Folio although it had appeared in 1609, 1611 and 1619; it was added to the Third Folio in 1664.

There was reluctance to publish plays at this time for various reasons: many plays were carelessly written for fast production; collaboration was frequent; plays were not really considered *reading* matter; they were sometimes circulated in manuscript; and the theatrical company, not the author, owned the rights. Those plays given individual publication appeared in a quarto, so named from the size of the page. A single sheet of paper was folded twice to make four leaves (thus *quarto*) or eight pages; these four leaves constitute one signature (one section of a bound book).

Authorized publication occurred when a company disbanded, when money was needed but rights were to be retained, when a play failed or ran into licensing difficulties (thus, hopefully, the printed work would justify the play against the criticism), or when a play had been pirated. Authorized editions are called good quartos. Piratical publication might occur when the manuscript of a play had circulated privately, when a member of a company desired money for himself, or when a stenographer or memorizer took the play down in the theater (such a version was recognizable by inclusion of stage directions derived from an eyewitness, by garbled sections, etc.). Pirated editions are called bad quartos. There are at least five bad quartos of Shakespeare's plays.

Authenticity of Works

Usually, 37 plays are printed in modern collections of Shakespeare's works, but some recent scholars have urged the addition of two more: *Edward III* and *Two Noble Kinsmen*. A case has also been advanced, unconvincingly, for a fragment of the play on Sir Thomas More. At times, six of the generally accepted plays have been questioned: *Henry VI,* Parts I, II and III, *Timon of Athens, Pericles* and *Henry VIII.* The first four are usually accepted today (one hopes all question concerning *Timon* has finally ended), but if Shakespeare did not write these plays in their entirety, he certainly wrote parts of them. Of course, collaboration in those days was commonplace. Aside from the two long narrative poems already mentioned and the sonnets (nos. 1-152, but not nos. 153-154), Shakespeare's poetic output is uncertain. *The Passionate Pilgrim* (1599) contains only five authenticated poems (two sonnets and three verses from *Love's Labour's Lost*), and *The Phoenix and the Turtle* (1601) may be his, but the authenticity of *A Lover's Complaint* (appended to the sonnets) is highly questionable.

Who Was Shakespeare?

At this point, we might mention a problem that has plagued Shakespeare study for over a century: who was Shakespeare? Those who would like to make the author of the plays someone else — Francis Bacon or the Earl of Oxford or even Christopher Marlowe (dead long before most of the plays were written) — have used the lack of information of Shakespeare's early years and the confusion in the evidence we have been examining to advance their candidate. But the major arguments against Shakespeare show the source of these speculators' disbelief to be in class snobbery and perhaps in a perverse adherence to minority opinion. The most common argument is that no one of Shakespeare's background, lack of education and lack of aristocratic experience could know all that the author knew. But study will reveal that such information was readily available in various popular sources, that some of it lies in the literary sources used for the play and that Shakespeare was probably not totally lacking in education or in social decorum. The more significant question of style and tone is not dealt with — nor could it successfully be raised. Bacon, for example, no matter how much we admire his mind and his writings, exhibits a writing style diametrically opposite to Shakespeare's, a style most unpoetic and often flat. The student would be wise not to waste time rehashing these unfounded theories. No such question was raised in the seventeenth or eighteenth centuries, and no serious student of the plays today doubts that Shakespeare *was* Shakespeare.

Shakespeare's England

The world of Elizabethan and Jacobean England was a world of growth and change. The great increase in the middle class, and in the population as a whole, demanded a new economy and means of livelihood, a new instrument of government (one recognizing "rights" and changed class structure), a new social code and a broad base of entertainment. The invention of printing a century before had contributed to that broader base, but it was the theater that supplied the more immediate needs of the greatest numbers. The theater grew and along with it came less educated, more money-conscious writers, who gave the people what they wanted: entertainment. But Shakespeare, having passed through a brief period of amateur writing, proceeded to set down important ideas in memorable language throughout most of his career. His plays, particularly the later ones, have been analyzed by recent critics in terms of literary quality through their metaphor, verse line, relationships with psychology and myth, and elaborate structure. Yet Shakespeare was a man of the stage, and the plays were written to be performed. Only this will fully account for the humor of a deadly serious play like *Hamlet* or the spectacle of a *Coriolanus*.

Life in London

During Shakespeare's early years there, London was a walled city of about 200,000, with seven gates providing access to the city from the east, north and west. It was geographically small and crisscrossed by narrow, little streets and lanes. The various wards each had a parish church that dominated the life of the close-knit community. To the south and outside were slums and the haunts of criminal types, and farther out were the agricultural lands and huge estates. As the population increased and the central area declined, the fashionable people of the city moved toward the west, where the palace of Westminster lay. Houses were generally rented out floor by floor and sometimes room by room. Slums were common within the city, too, though close to pleasant enough streets and squares. "Merrie Olde England" was not really clean, nor were its people, for in those days there were no sewers or drains except the gutter in the middle of the street, into which garbage would be emptied to be floated off by the rain to Fleet ditch or Moor ditch. Plague was particularly ravaging from 1592 to 1594 (when the theaters were closed to avoid contamination) and 1603. Medical knowledge, of course, was slight; ills were "cured" by amputation, leeching, bloodletting and cathartics. The city was (and still is) dominated by St. Paul's Cathedral, around which booksellers clustered on Paternoster Row.

Religious Atmosphere

Of great significance for the times was religion. Under Elizabeth, a state church had developed. It was Protestant in nature and was called Anglican (or today, Episcopalian) but it had arisen from Henry VIII's break with the pope and from a compromise with the Roman Catholics, who had gained power under Mary Tudor.

The Church of England was headed by the Archbishop of Canterbury, who was to be an increasingly important figure in the early part of the seventeenth century. There were also many schismatic groups, which generally desired further departures from Roman Catholicism. Calvinists were perhaps the most numerous and important of the Protestant groups. The Puritans, who were Calvinist, desired to "purify" the church of ritual and certain dogmas, but during the 1590s they were lampooned as extremists in dress and conduct.

Political Milieu

During Shakespeare's lifetime there were two monarchs: Elizabeth I, 1558-1603, and James I, 1603-1625. Elizabeth was the daughter of Henry VIII and Anne Boleyn, his second wife, who was executed in 1536. After Henry's death, his son by his third wife, Jane Seymour (died in 1537), reigned as Edward VI. He was followed by Mary Tudor, daughter of Henry's first wife, Catherine of Aragon. Mary was a Roman Catholic, who tried to put down religious dissension by persecution of both Protestants and Catholics. Nor did her marriage to Philip II of Spain endear her to the people.

Elizabeth's reign was troubled by many offers of marriage, particularly from Spanish and French nobles — all Roman Catholic — and by the people's concern for an heir to the throne. English suitors generally cancelled one another out by intrigue or aggressiveness. One of the most prominent was the Earl of Essex, Robert Devereux, who fell in and out of favor.

He apparently attempted to take over the reins of control, only to be captured, imprisoned and executed in February, 1601. One claimant to the throne was Mary of Scotland, a Roman Catholic and widow of Francis II of France. She was the second cousin of Elizabeth, tracing her claim through her grandmother, who was Henry VIII's sister. Finally, settlement came with Elizabeth's acceptance of Mary's son as heir apparent, though Mary was to be captured, tried and executed for treason in 1587. Mary had abdicated the throne of Scotland in 1567 in favor of her son, James VI. His ascent to the throne of England in 1603 as James I joined the two kingdoms for the first time, although Scotland during the seventeenth century often acted independently of England.

Contemporary Events

Political and religious problems were intermingled in the celebrated Gunpowder Plot. Angry over fines that were levied upon those not attending Church of England services — primarily Roman Catholics — and offended by difficulties over papal envoys, a group of Catholics plotted to blow up Parliament, and James with it, at its first session on November 5, 1605. A cache of gunpowder was stored in the cellar, guarded by various conspirators, among them Guy Fawkes. The plot was discovered before it could be carried out and Fawkes, on duty at the time, was apprehended. The execution of the plotters and the triumph of the anti-Papists led in succeeding years to celebrations in the streets and the hanging of Fawkes in effigy.

Among the most noteworthy public events during these times were the wars with the Spanish, which included the defeat of the Spanish Armada in 1588, the battle in the Lowlands in 1590-1594, the expedition to Cadiz under Essex in 1596 and the expedition to the Azores (the Islands Expedition), also under Essex, in 1597. With trading companies especially set up for colonization and exploitation, travel excited the imagination of the people: here was a new way of life, here were new customs brought back by the sailors and merchants, here was a new dreamworld to explore.

In all, the years from around 1590 to 1601 were trying ones for English people, relieved only by the news from abroad, the new affluence and the hope for the future under James. Writers of the period frequently reflect, however, the disillusionment and sadness of those difficult times.

9

The Elizabethan Theater

Appearance

The Elizabethan playhouse developed from the medieval inn with its rooms grouped around a courtyard into which a stage was built. This pattern was used in The Theatre, built by James Burbage in 1576: a square frame building (later round or octagonal) with a square yard, three tiers of galleries, each jutting out over the one below, and a stage extending into the middle of the yard, where people stood or sat on improvised seats. There was no cover over the yard or stage, and lighting was therefore natural. Thus, performances were what we might consider late matinees or early evening performances.

Other theaters were constructed during the ensuing years: The Curtain in 1577, The Rose in 1587 (on Bankside), The Swan in 1595 (also Bankside) and Shakespeare's playhouse, The Globe, in 1599 (not far from The Rose). There is still some question about the exact dimensions of this house, but it seems to have been octagonal, each side measuring about 36 feet, with an over-all diameter of 84 feet. It was about 33 feet to the eaves, and the yard was 56 feet in diameter. Three sides were used for backstage and to serve the needs of the players. There was no curtain or proscenium, hence the spectators became part of the action. Obviously, the actors' asides and soliloquies were effective under these conditions.

There was no real scenery and there were only a few major props. Thus, the lines of the play had to reveal locations and movement, changes in time or place, etc. In this way, too, it was easier to establish a nonrealistic setting, for all settings were created in words. On either side of the stage were doors, within the flooring were trapdoors (for entrances of ghosts, etc.), and behind the main stage was the inner stage or recess. Here, indoor scenes (such as a court or a bedchamber) were played, and some props could be used because the inner stage was usually concealed by a curtain when not in use. It might also have served to hide someone behind the ever-present arras, like Polonius in *Hamlet*. The "chamber" was on the second level, with windows and a balcony. On the third level was another chamber, primarily for musicians.

Actors

An acting company such as the Lord Chamberlain's Men was a fellowship of ten to 15 sharers with some ten to 12 extras, three or four boys (often to play women's roles) who might become full sharers and stagehands. There were rival companies, each with its leading dramatist and leading tragic actor and clown. The Lord Admiral's Men, organized in 1594, boasted Ben Jonson and the tragedian, Edward Alleyn. Some of the rivalry of this War of the Theaters is reflected in the speeches of Hamlet, who also comments on the ascendancy and unwarranted popularity of the children's companies (like the Children of Blackfriars) in the late 1590s.

The company dramatist, of course, had to think in terms of the members of his company as he wrote his play. He had to make use of the physical features and peculiar talents of the actors, making sure, besides, that there was a role for each member. The fact that women's parts were taken by boys imposed obvious limitations on the range of action. Accordingly, we often find women characters impersonating men. For example, Robert Goffe played Portia in *The Merchant of Venice,* and Portia impersonates a male lawyer in the important trial scene. Goffe also played Juliet, Anne in *Richard III* and Oberon in *A Midsummer Night's Dream.* The influence of an actor on the playwright can be seen, on the one hand, by noting the "humor" characters portrayed so competently by Thomas Pope, who was a choleric Mercutio in *Romeo,* a melancholic Jaques in *As You Like It* and a sanguinary Falstaff in *Henry IV,* Part 1; and by comparing, on the other hand, the clown, Bottom, in *A Midsummer Night's Dream,* played in a frolicsome manner by William Kempe, with the clown, Feste, in *Twelfth Night,* sung and danced by Robert Armin. Obviously, too, if a certain kind of character was not available within the company, then that kind of character could not be written into the play. The approach was decidedly different from ours today, where the play almost always comes first and the casting of roles second. The plays were performed in a repertory system, with a different play each afternoon. The average life of a play was about ten performances.

History of the Drama

English drama goes back to native forms developed from playlets presented at church holidays. Mystery plays dealt with biblical stories such as the Nativity or the Passion, and miracle plays usually depicted the lives of saints. The merchant and craft guilds that came to own and produce the cycles of plays were the forerunners of the theatrical companies of Shakespeare's time. The kind of production these cycles received, either as moving pageants in the streets or as staged shows in a churchyard, influenced the late sixteenth-century production of secular plays, in that there was an intimacy with the audience and there was a great reliance on words rather than setting and props. Similar involvement with the stage action is experienced by audiences of the arena theater of today.

The morality play, the next form to develop, was an allegory of the spiritual conflict between good and evil in the soul of man. The *dramatis personae* were abstract virtues and vices, with at least one man representing Mankind (or Everyman, as the most popular of these plays was titled). Some modern critics see *Othello* as a kind of morality play in which the soul of Othello is vied for by the aggressively evil Iago (as a kind of Satanic figure) and passively good Desdemona (as a personification of Christian faith in all men). The Tudor interlude — a short, witty, visual play — may have influenced the subplot of the Elizabethan play with its jesting and visual tricks. In mid-sixteenth century appeared the earliest known English comedies, Nicholas Udall's *Ralph Roister Doister* and *Gammer Gurton's Needle* (of uncertain authorship). Both show the influence of the Roman comic playwright, Plautus. Shakespeare's *Comedy of Errors,* performed in the 1590s, was an adaptation of Plautus' *Menaechmi,* both plays featuring twins and an involved story of confused identities. Senecan tragedy is a tragedy of revenge, characterized by many deaths, much bloodletting, ghosts, feigned madness and the motif of a death for a death.

Shakespeare's Artistry

Plots

Generally, a Shakespearean play has two plots: a main plot and a subplot. The subplot reflects the main plot and is often concerned with inferior characters. Two contrasting examples will suffice. In *King Lear*, Lear and his daughters furnish the characters for the main plot of filial love and ingratitude, whereas Gloucester and his sons enact the same theme in the subplot. Lear and Gloucester both learn that outward signs of love may be false. In *A Midsummer Night's Dream,* the town workmen (Quince, Bottom *et al.*) put on a tragic play in such a hilarious way that it turns the subject of the play — love so strong that the hero will kill himself if his loved one dies first — into farce, but this, in the main plot, is the "serious" plight of the four mixed-up lovers. In both examples Shakespeare has reinforced his points by subplots dealing with the same subject as the main plot.

Sources

The plots of the Elizabethan plays were usually adapted from other sources. Originality was not the sought quality; a kind of variation on a theme was. It was felt that one could better evaluate the playwright's worth by seeing what he did with a familiar tale. What he stressed, how he stressed it, how he restructured the familiar elements — these were the important matters. Shakespeare closely followed Sir Thomas North's very popular translation of Plutarch's *Life of Marcus Antonius,* for example, in writing *Antony and Cleopatra*; and he modified Robert Greene's *Pandosto* and combined it with the Pygmalion myth in *The Winter's Tale,* while drawing the character of Autolycus from certain pamphlets written by Greene. The only plays for which sources have not been clearly determined are *Love's Labour's Lost* (probably based on contemporary events) and *The Tempest* (possibly based on some shipwreck account from travellers to the New World).

Verse and Prose

There is a mixture of verse and prose in the plays, partially because plays fully in verse were out of fashion. Greater variety could thus be achieved and character or atmosphere could be more precisely delineated. Elevated passages, philosophically significant ideas and speeches by men of high rank are in verse, but comic and light parts, speeches including dialect or broken English, and scenes that move more rapidly or simply give mundane information are in prose. The poetry is almost always blank verse (iambic pentameter lines without rhyme). Rhyme is used, however (particularly the couplet), to mark the close of scenes or an important action. Rhyme also serves as a cue for the entrance of another actor or some off-stage business, to point to a change of mood or thought, as a forceful opening after a passage of prose, to convey excitement, passion or sentimentality, and to distinguish characters.

Shakespeare's plays may be divided into three general categories, though some plays are not readily classified and further subdivisions may be suggested within a category.

The History Play

The history play, or chronicle, may tend to tragedy, like *Richard II,* or to comedy, like *Henry IV,* Part I. It is a chronicle of some royal personage, often altered for dramatic purposes, even to the point of falsification of the facts. Its popularity may have resulted from the rise of nationalism, nurtured by the successes against the Spanish, the developing trade and colonization, and England's rising prestige as a world power. The chronicle was considered a political guide, like the popular *Mirror for Magistrates,* a collection of writings showing what happens when an important leader falls through some error in his ways, his thinking or his personality. Thus, the history play counselled the right path by negative, if not positive, means. Accordingly, it is difficult to call *Richard II* a tragedy, since Richard was wrong and his wrongness harmed his people. The political philosophy of Shakespeare's day seemed to favor the view that all usurpation was bad and should be corrected, but not by further usurpation. When that original usurpation had been established, through an heir's ascension to the throne, it was to be accepted. Then any rebellion against the "true" king would be a rebellion against God.

Tragedy

Tragedy, in simple terms, meant that the protagonist died. Certain concepts drawn from Aristotle's *Poetics* require a tragic hero of high standing, who must oppose some conflicting force, either external or internal. The tragic hero should be dominated by a *hamartia* (a so-called tragic flaw, but really an *excess* of some character trait, e.g., pride or *hubris*), and it is this *hamartia* that leads to his downfall and, because of his status, to the downfall of others. The action presented in the tragedy must be recognizable to the audience as real. Through seeing it enacted, the audience has its passion (primarily, suffering) raised, and the conclusion of the action thus brings release from that passion (*catharsis*). A more meaningful way of looking at tragedy in the Elizabethan theater, however, is to see it as that which occurs when essential good (like Hamlet) is wasted (through disaster or death) in the process of driving out evil (such as Claudius represents).

Comedy

Comedy, in simple terms, meant that the play ended happily for the protagonists. Sometimes the comedy depends on exaggerations of man's eccentricities — comedy of humors; sometimes the comedy is romantic and far-fetched. The romantic comedy was usually based on a mix-up in events or confused identity of characters, particularly by disguise. It moved toward tragedy in that an important person might die and the mix-up might never be unravelled. But, in the nick of time, something happens or someone appears (sometimes illogically or unexpectedly) and saves the day. It reflects the structure of myth by moving from happiness to despair to resurrection. *The Winter's Tale* is a perfect example of this, for the happiness of the first part is banished with Hermione's exile and Perdita's abandonment; tragedy is near when the lost baby, Perdita, cannot be found and Hermione is presumed dead. But Perdita reappears, as does Hermione, a statue that suddenly comes to life. Lost identities are established and confusions disappear, but the mythic-comic nature of the play is seen in the reuniting of the mother, Hermione, a kind of Ceres, with her daughter, Perdita, a kind of Proserpina. Spring returns, summer will bring the harvest and the winter of the tale is left behind — for a little while.

THE TAMING OF THE SHREW
Sources

The main difficulty presented by any consideration of the
sources Shakespeare used in writing *The Taming of the Shrew* lies
in the existence of an anonymous play, printed in 1594, and en-
titled *The Taming of a Shrew*. Although this text is a badly
printed one and differs in many ways from Shakespeare's, it does
deal with the same story in roughly the same manner and has
many incidental similarities.

The principal scholarly theories concerning the relationship
between the two plays may be conveniently summarized as
follows: (1) that *A Shrew* was Shakespeare's source, and that he
wrote his play either alone or in collaboration with some other
writer; (2) that *A Shrew* and Shakespeare's play were based on a
common earlier play or tale on the same theme, which has since
been lost; (3) that *A Shrew* is an abridged version of
Shakespeare's play, perhaps reconstructed from memory by a
small travelling company of actors. Probably the most conven-
ient way of treating the details of the relationship between these
two plays, as well as of describing the other materials
Shakespeare may have used, is to deal with each of the three plot
strands separately.

The Petruchio-Katharina Plot

The main plot derives from a large body of popular
literature devoted to the war between the sexes for mastery in
marriage, a theme that stretches back to classical times. In Euro-
pean literature before the Age of Elizabeth, the theme had been
treated frequently. Among the more popular English versions of
it were the "Wife of Bath's Prologue" and "Tale," the "Merchant's Tale" and the "Clerk's Tale" in Chaucer's *Canterbury
Tales* (c. 1380-1400), some stories in *A Hundred Merry Tales*
(1525), *Tales and Quick Answers* (1567), *the Jests of Scoggin*,
King Henry IV's jester, (printed 1565-66) and *The Ballad of the
Curst Wife* (1550).

In its treatment of the main plot, *A Shrew* has in common
with Shakespeare's play a number of incidents and characters: (1)
Ferando (Petruchio) announces his intention to marry Alfonso's
(Baptista's) eldest daughter by treating her to as much scolding as
she inflicts upon others (see Act I, Scene 2); (2) Kate is willing to
marry Ferando because she is attracted to him despite herself (see

Act II, Scene 1); (3) Her shrewish fury is displayed when Valeria attempts to teach her to play the lute (see Act II, Scene 1); (4) Ferando comes to the wedding wildly dressed and merely praises Kate when she complains of his outrageous behavior. He refuses to stay for the wedding feast and takes her to his home against her will. His friends speculate about the outcome of their marriage (see Act III, Scene 2); (5) Ferando behaves badly to his servants, throws about the food that has been prepared for him and assures the audience that he intends to tame Kate by depriving her of food and rest (see Act IV, Scene 1); (6) Kate is tormented with the promise of food by Sander (Grumio), Ferando's servant (see Act IV, Scene 3); (7) Ferando prepares food for Kate, allows her to have it on his conditions and finds fault with the clothes she needs for her sister's wedding (see Act IV, Scene 3); (8) Ferando often tests Kate's obedience by making her say that it is the time of the day that he insists it to be. On the journey to her father's house, he forces her to agree with what he says about the sun and about an old man they meet on the highway (see Act IV, Scene 5); (9) At the wedding feast, Ferando bets on Kate's obedience. Kate throws her cap underfoot at his command and forcibly brings in two brides, to whom she delivers a long speech on the proper duty of a wife to her husband (see Act V, Scene 2).

Although Shakespeare's treatment of the events in *The Shrew* is remarkably similar to that found in *A Shrew*, the difference between the two plays lies in the quality of writing and characterization. Petruchio is a much more rounded and fully humanized character than Ferando, and his speech is more polished, colorful and vital. Shakespeare's Katharina is also more believable in her behavior and motivation and she is less crude in her speech than her namesake in *A Shrew*. Grumio, too, is a far more attractive and genuinely individualized comic creation than Sander, who is little more than a stereotyped immoral and impertinent manservant.

The Lucentio-Bianca Plot

Shakespeare's handling of the material in the subplot is far more refined and dramatically direct than its treatment in *A Shrew*. In *A Shrew*, Kate has two younger sisters, Emelye (Bianca) and Phylena, neither of whom may be wooed until Kate is wed. Two young men, Polidor and Aurelius (Lucentio), fall in love with them and decide to disguise themselves in order to pursue their courtship. Other events similar to those in Shakespeare's play include Aurelius' servant, Valeria (Tranio), assuming his master's identity to deal with Alfonso (Baptista), the procuring of a merchant, Phylotus (the Pedant), to pretend to be Aurelius' father, the meeting on the highway between Aurelius' real father, the Duke of Cestus (Vincentio), and Ferando (Petruchio) and Kate, and Aurelius' suggestion at his marriage feast that the husbands wager on their wives' obedience.

In his treatment of the subplot, Shakespeare was probably influenced a good deal by a neoclassical comedy, George Gascoigne's *The Supposes* (1566), which is an English prose version of Lodovico Ariosto's Italian play, *I Suppositi* (1509). In Gascoigne's work, he found the names Petruchio and Licio, two servants in the play. Gascoigne's hero, Erostrato, like Lucentio, changes places with his servant to gain access to his mistress. There are also an old man, Cleander (Gremio), who is the hero's rival in love, a merchant (the Pedant), who pretends to be the hero's father, and the episodes of the secret marriage and final reconciliation between father and son.

The Christopher Sly Framework Plot

The basic situation in the framework material, a beggar persuaded he is a lord, is of very ancient origin and has been traced back as far as the *Arabian Nights*. Since there were many versions of the story in English and French literature before Shakespeare's time, it is impossible to determine exactly from which treatment of it either Shakespeare or the author of *A Shrew* gained his knowledge of the motif.

Shakespeare's Induction is about twice the length of the one in *A Shrew*, and Shakespeare's is infinitely richer in accurate human observation, in its relevance to the inset play and in its skilful comic prose. In *A Shrew*, it is a tapster rather than a hostess who ejects the drunken Sly from the alehouse at the opening, and the tinker does not disappear early in the play as he does in Shakespeare's. There are four short exchanges as Sly interrupts the play, and there is a final scene showing him back where he was found, in front of the alehouse, talking to the tapster about his wonderful dream and about his intention of applying Petruchio's methods to the taming of his own shrewish wife.

18

The Problem of Authorship

Closely connected with the problem of the relationship between *The Taming of a Shrew* and Shakespeare's play is the controversy concerning the authenticity of the text found in the First Folio. Scholars have debated for over 100 years whether it is by Shakespeare alone or whether it is the product of some kind of collaboration between him and another dramatist.

In general, those scholars who have supported the collaboration theory have divided the play as follows: the Induction and the scenes dealing solely with Petruchio and Katharina have been attributed to Shakespeare, and the scenes dealing with the wooing of Bianca have been considered the work of a collaborator. More precise divisions of the play have been attempted.

No very accurate tests in support of the collaboration theory have been offered. The main argument in its favor has been the impression of inferior verse in the supposedly non-Shakespearean sections. More specifically, some critics have cited: (1) the overuse of Italian and Latin dialogue and of classical allusions; (2) careless slips in plot structure; (3) the presence of certain words never used elsewhere in Shakespeare's writing; (4) rhythmic irregularities in the emphasis placed on unimportant words and the lack of uniformity in pronunciation. The collaborator has been variously identified as Thomas Lodge, Robert Greene, Samuel Rowley or George Chapman.

The advocates of Shakespeare's sole authorship of the play have attacked the evidence of their opponents, showing that none of the four kinds of criteria cited by those favoring the collaboration theory really stands up to close examination in the light of Shakespeare's practice in his other plays.

It has also been demonstrated that the close connection, thematically and physically, between the two plots in the play makes it unlikely that the play was the product of two authors. For example, the two final scenes of the play, which are constructed around a juxtaposition of the two marriages and which involve characters from both plots, make the two-author hypothesis difficult to believe.

The presentation of characters throughout the play has also been analyzed, and it has been argued that there is a consistency and unity in their portrayal in the Shakespearean and reputedly non-Shakespearean sections.

In recent years, some scholars have examined the patterns of imagery in the play against similar ones found in other accepted Shakespearean plays. All of them have come to the conclusion that, while such evidence of authorship can never be final, all parts of *The Taming of the Shrew* contain image clusters that are characteristic of Shakespeare or are similar to his practice elsewhere in his works.

The Framework Device

The device of "framing" a play with some other dramatic material was a common one in the Elizabethan theater. Its use has been noted in some forty-five plays of the period. There has been some disagreement among scholars, however, as to whether or not the framework material as it appears in the Folio text of *The Taming of the Shrew* represents Shakespeare's final intentions. On the one hand, it has been argued that the playwright, after his elaborate treatment of Sly in the Induction, would have supplied some scene at the end of the play showing the tinker's removal from the lord's house and his awakening at the alehouse door, perhaps similar to that found in the anonymous *The Taming of a Shrew*. Against this view is the opinion that the play is better as it stands, that Shakespeare planned to remove Sly from the stage once the audience's attention was fixed on the inset play and that a final scene dealing with Sly's affairs would have been an anticlimax after the conclusion of the play proper in Act V, Scene 2.

There are good critical arguments for both these points of view. Whichever theory one agrees with will ultimately depend upon one's aesthetic judgment of the play as a whole. Certainly, so far as stage production of the piece is concerned, both the ending as we have it and the adding on of the final scene of *A Shrew* have been equally effective. However, it should be noted that Richard Hosley's study of the use of the framework device in the drama of the period indicates that over half of the plays containing such material lack a final scene. Further, owing to the necessity for members of the relatively small acting companies of the time to assume more than one role, actors would not always have been available after taking part in the last scene of the play proper, which often brought together all of the leading players.

Despite critical controversy over the framework material, it is generally agreed upon that there is a close thematic connection between the Induction and the inset play. Both Katharina and Sly are the subject of an experiment in the manipulation of human personality. While Sly has lost his senses and reason through drink, Kate has lost hers through inflated pride. Both Petruchio and the lord attempt to test the resistance of their victims' states of mind against the powers of sustained imagination, the latter with his play, and the former with a performance worthy of any actor. Just as Kate becomes like one awakened from a dream of shrewishness, so Sly, after experiencing the reality of the stage world, is reluctant to fall back again into his dream of drunkenness.

Classical and Romance Elements

Two basic forms of comedy were apparently recognized by Elizabethan playwrights. These are usually known as classical, or intrigue, comedy and romantic, or narrative, comedy.

The classical type is satirical in intention and was derived from Latin models or from English imitations of them. The characters are traditional types, and the plots are usually centered on some obstacle to happiness posed by a money-minded father or jealous husband, or on the separation of lovers or parents and children. The action includes a great deal of intrigue and misunderstanding that is often the result of the manipulations of a clever servant or cunning troublemaker. The complications of plot are usually worked out in the final scene in a sudden or unexpected development.

The romantic, or narrative, type of comedy is of mixed origins. It often combines elements of classical plays with those of English folk plays, medieval farces, civic pageants, Italian tragicomedy, pastoral plays and poems and the full-length prose and verse romances. The aim of these plays is to tell a story, generally of romantic love and its trials, but they often include a variety of comical, pastoral or supernatural situations.

The Taming of the Shrew contains elements of both of these kinds of comedy.

Classical Elements

Apart from the scenes on the country road and at Petruchio's country house, the setting of *The Taming of the Shrew*, as is true of most classical comedies, is urban and bourgeois. There is a high proportion of elderly characters, four of the main ones being old men: Gremio, Baptista, Vincentio and the pedant. Two of these are deceived fathers who are intent on their offsprings making financially good marriages. The other two — Gremio and the pedant — are stock figures drawn from Latin comedy, the former even being called "a pantaloon" in a stage direction. Katharina is basically the stock figure of the shrewish wife and Petruchio is the blustering, self-confident husband. Both of these types are familiar figures in classical plays. Tranio's part in the intrigue of the subplot is reminiscent of that of the witty servant of the classical play.

The attitude toward marriage that is expressed in the play is to a large extent Roman for, as in classical Roman comedy, many characters give evidence of viewing matrimony as primarily an economic and social institution rather than as the logical end of romantic love. For example, Petruchio initially makes wealth "the burden of his wooing dance" and urges Baptista to a speedy legal and financial settlement. The pedant also knows in Act IV, Scene 4 how to strike the right note of business transaction in discussing Lucentio's marriage. Baptista, too, makes it quite clear in Act II, Scene 1 that his chief concern in marrying off his beloved Bianca is a financial one. Finally, Hortensio is obviously greatly taken with the wealth of the widow he weds after his failure to win Bianca.

The subplot is full of the complicated disguise and love intrigue typical of the classical plays, where the young often deceive their elders. Grumio's line, "See, to beguile the old folks, how the young folks lay their heads together!" is both an appropriate comment on the action in Act I, Scene 2 and a good brief definition of the typical classical comic plot.

There is also a great deal of slapstick humor in the play, a feature which, again, is typical of the genre. For example, notice Petruchio's ill-treatment of his servants in Act II, Scene 1 and in Act IV, Scene 1; Katharina's baiting of Bianca in Act II, Scene 1, and her own manhandling by Petruchio during their first encounter; the reported scenes of violent comedy on the journey from Padua in Act IV, Scene 1 and at the outrageous wedding in Act III, Scene 2.

Romance Elements

Certain aspects of the play prevent our viewing it as a purely classical comedy. For example, there is some evidence of a very different concept of love and marriage in the Lucentio-Bianca plot — one which is much nearer to that normally found in romantic comedy. Lucentio pursues his mistress regardless of economic and social considerations and he intends marriage rather than sexual conquest from the outset. He falls in love at first sight and records the effects of his passion in Petrarchan love-lyric style. This romantic note is not sustained, however, and there is no central romantic love scene between the two.

The romantic attitude toward love is even evident in the main plot. Many critics, who have seen in the Petruchio-Katharina relationship the signs of a growing affection between them, claim that Shakespeare was interested in a developing romantic attachment rather than in a brutal display of shrew-taming.

The Induction material, too, has an atmosphere more in keeping with romantic than classical comedy. Its basically rural setting, its references to hunting, its fairy-tale situation and its three-dimensional character depiction are all romantic elements.

Elizabethan Attitudes Toward Marriage

The Taming of the Shrew is a play about marriage, a topic on which the original audience would have had certain preconceptions that are very different from the ideas that prevail today.

Most of the factual information concerning marriage customs of the Elizabethan period is related to the practices of the middle and upper classes of the time. From this body of evidence, it is apparent that many members of Shakespeare's audience would have sympathized with Baptista's situation in the play and with his method of dealing with it. It was considered proper for marriages to be arranged by parents, and it was a matter of social duty for a father to ensure that his daughters were provided with husbands of appropriate financial and social status.

The attitudes of other characters in the play are similarly in accord with the practices of the time. Many young men, like Petruchio, were apparently willing to take advantage of the prevailing state of affairs and marry for money. Matches between young girls and wealthy, established old men were also sufficiently common to make Gremio's expectation of success with Bianca quite credible. Thus, the basic situation in the piece is a realistic rather than a farcical one.

Although the arranged marriage was the usual custom, there was a certain amount of opposition to it on religious grounds, for it was seen to stimulate parental greed and, on romantic grounds, because it led to marital unhappiness or, at best, to unions lacking in love. As a result of this antagonism to the prevailing system, parents were making some concessions to the inclinations of their children. An echo of this parental indulgence may be found in Baptista's remark to Petruchio in Act II, Scene 1 that their business arrangement concerning Katharina's hand will be clinched "when the special thing is well obtained,/This is, her love; for that is all in all."

Because of its relationship to real life, the play can be viewed as a dramatic commentary on contemporary marriage. Petruchio is fundamentally a follower of the old school of thought, for he thinks of his wife as:

> . . . my goods, my chattels . . . my house,

My household stuff, my field, my barn,
My horse, my ox, my ass, my anything.
                                      (Act III, Scene 2, 226-228)

In his attitudes, Petruchio is contrasted with Bianca's two love-sick suitors, Lucentio and Hortensio, who, in fine romantic fashion, set their mistress on a pedestal, far removed from the considerations of marital economics.

Katharina and her younger sister are contrasted in a similar manner. Both revolt in their different ways against their society's assumption that the subjection of women is natural. One rebels openly and shrewishly, while the other assumes a surface submission that serves to cover the deception and intrigue necessary to get her own way. However, as the two plots develop, the initial characters of the two girls undergo a reversal, so that the defiant shrew of the opening scenes becomes the perfect wife, while the sweet, submissive daughter, during the same period of time, works up to a wifely display of a very independent will.

In the treatment of Baptista and Gremio, there is certainly some criticism of arranged marriages based primarily on financial considerations. But there is also, in the presentation of Lucentio and Bianca's relationship, some implicit satire at the expense of the deceitful kind of courtship that is based on highly romantic attitudes and on ignoring the realities of existence. The play's ultimate judgment would appear to be in favor of the hard-won relationship founded on knowledge and experience and existing within the marriage conventions of the time. Such a relationship is exemplified, ironically, by Petruchio and his tamed shrew.

Plot Summary

Induction

Christopher Sly, a drunken tinker, is picked up by a nobleman and his friends, who are eager for a practical joke. They dress the drunkard in fine clothes, put him in a beautifully furnished room in the lord's castle and, when he awakens, try to convince him that he is a nobleman who has been insane for fifteen years. For Sly's entertainment, a play, *The Taming of the Shrew,* is put on.

The Taming of the Shrew

Baptista Minola, a wealthy merchant of Padua, has two unmarried daughters. The elder has a fiery temper and is a sharp-tongued woman known as Katharina the Shrew. The younger sister, Bianca, gentle and attractive, cannot be married until her sister has found a husband.

Although Bianca already has two suitors, Gremio and Hortensio, a third one soon appears. He is young Lucentio of Pisa, who has come to Padua to study. He falls in love with Bianca at first sight, and plots to gain access to her by posing as a tutor of Latin and Greek. His affection is soon returned. Tranio, his servant, assumes his master's clothes and duties while Lucentio is occupied with lovemaking.

Hortensio and Gremio, rivals for Bianca's hand, agree to work together on one project: to find a husband for Katharina. Soon after this agreement, Petruchio arrives in the city and seeks out his friend, Hortensio.

Petruchio, wealthy already but interested in increasing his capital, willingly consents to woo Katharina. He courts her in violent fashion, sweeping aside all her objections and disregarding her angry outbursts. He then leaves for Venice, supposedly to purchase wedding clothes. He promises to return on Sunday, the date set for the marriage.

Sunday comes and so does Petruchio — late and in strange apparel, mounted on a mangy old nag and followed by his servant Grumio, also in comic dress. Baptista cannot persuade his prospective son-in-law to change to suitable clothes. The wedding ceremony is performed, but the groom stirs up so much excitement that the priest drops his book.

Meanwhile, the romance of Lucentio and Bianca has made

progress. Tranio, in his role of Lucentio, distracts the attention of Baptista from what is actually happening by outwardly courting Bianca himself. He is challenged by Gremio, who has her father's permission to marry Bianca the Sunday after her sister's wedding, unless the supposed Lucentio can present her with a larger dowry. Tranio now has to make good his extravagant boasts of wealth by finding a man to impersonate Vincentio of Pisa, father of the real Lucentio. An old pedant, journeying to Florence on business, is persuaded to act the part. Bianca's father is therefore kept occupied until the couple can elope.

Immediately after the wedding, Petruchio carries Kate away with him on the broken-down horse. A rough journey brings them to Petruchio's country house, where excited servants are cursed and kicked and where Kate is not permitted either food or rest. Petruchio orders new and elegant clothes for Kate, but finds fault with them and scornfully says that they will both wear their old clothes back to Padua. He dismisses the tailor and the haberdasher who are, however, paid later.

Hortensio, having abandoned his suit of Bianca in favor of a wealthy widow, has gone to Petruchio's house to attend the taming school before venturing into marriage. He accompanies the newlyweds on a memorable trip back to Padua, where Petruchio forces his bride to call the sun the moon and an old man they meet on the road a "fresh budding virgin."

This old man is the real Vincentio, on his way to Padua to see his son. Soon he discovers the two imposters, Tranio and the pedant, in the house of Lucentio and thinks that his son has been robbed and murdered. Just as Vincentio is about to have the impersonators arrested, the real Lucentio and his bride, Bianca, appear and ask a blessing of both fathers. Baptista has, by this time, joined the group.

Now thoroughly tamed, Kate is summoned after dinner to explain to the other two brides — Bianca and the Widow — their duties toward their husbands. This she does so completely to Petruchio's satisfaction that he rewards her with:

Why, there's a wench! Come on and kiss me, Kate!

Amid uproarious laughter, the play comes to an end.

Characters in the Play

Characters in the Induction

A LORD: He finds the drunken tinker, Christopher Sly, whom he takes home and persuades that he is a nobleman. The lord employs the actors who perform *The Taming of the Shrew* for Sly.

A HOSTESS: When Sly gets drunk in her alehouse at the beginning of the play, she drives him out.

CHRISTOPHER SLY: A drunken tinker, who is found by the lord asleep outside an alehouse. He is taken to the lord's house, dressed in fine clothes and persuaded by the lord and his servants that he is a nobleman who has been afflicted with madness.

BARTHOLOMEW: The lord's page, he dresses as a girl to pretend he is Sly's wife.

PLAYERS: A group of actors employed by the lord to perform *The Taming of the Shrew* for Christopher Sly.

SERVANTS: Retainers of the lord. They assist in deceiving Sly.

HUNTSMEN: The train of men accompanying the lord when he finds Sly.

Characters in the Play of *The Taming of the Shrew*

BAPTISTA: A wealthy gentleman of Padua and the father of Katharina and Bianca.

KATHARINA: Baptista's elder daughter, who has a reputation for being a shrew, and whom Petruchio marries and tames during the course of the play.

BIANCA: Baptista's younger daughter, whom he favors over Katharina. Gremio and Hortensio desire to marry her, but she falls in love with and marries Lucentio.

GREMIO: A rich old gentleman of Padua. One of the suitors for Bianca's hand, he employs Lucentio (disguised as Cambio) as a schoolmaster for her.

HORTENSIO: A young man in love with Bianca. He disguises himself as a music master, Licio, in order to court her.

LUCENTIO: A young man from Pisa who, on a visit to Padua, falls in love with Bianca. He exchanges roles with his servant, Tranio, and disguises himself as Cambio, a schoolmaster, so that he may secretly court Bianca.

TRANIO: A servant of Lucentio's. He assumes his master's identity while Lucentio is disguised as a schoolmaster.

BIONDELLO: A foolish servant of Lucentio's.

VINCENTIO: An old gentleman of Pisa and Lucentio's father. He visits his son in Padua at the end of the play.

PETRUCHIO: A young gentleman of Verona who courts and marries Katharina and sets out to cure her of her schrewishnes during the course of the play.

GRUMIO: A servant of Petruchio's who aids his master in his plans for taming Katharina.

CURTIS: An old servant in charge of Petruchio's country house.

NATHANIEL, PHILIP, JOSEPH, NICHOLAS, PETER: Servants of Petruchio at his country house.

A PEDANT: An old man of Mantua who is persuaded by Tranio and Lucentio to pretend he is Lucentio's father.

A WIDOW: A wealthy woman who marries Hortensio at the end of the play.

A TAILOR: A tradesman employed by Petruchio to design a gown for Katharina.

A HABERDASHER: A tradesman employed by Petruchio to make a cap for Katharina.

Summaries and Commentaries
by Act and Scene

INDUCTION 1

Summary

The door of an alehouse on a Warwickshire heath is flung open and a drunken tinker, Christopher Sly, is driven, staggering, out by the hostess. She severely scolds Sly and demands that he pay for the glasses he has broken. He refuses to do so and proceeds to fall asleep under a bush, while the hostess exits to summon the constable. The sound of a hunting horn is heard, and a lord enters with his huntsmen and servants. They are disputing among themselves the relative merits of various hunting dogs. Just as the lord is ordering that his animals be attended to, in preparation for another hunt the following day, he catches sight of Sly and asks one of the servants to determine whether the tinker is dead or drunk. Learning that the tinker breathes, he decides he will take Sly to his house and persuade him he is a nobleman by dressing him in expensive clothes, putting rings on his fingers and setting a delicious banquet by his bedside.

The lord gives instructions on exactly how Sly is to be treated. He orders his servants to place the beggar in the finest chamber in the house, which is to be hung about with "wanton pictures." His head is to be bathed, and musicians are to be ready to play to him when he awakens. The servants are also to carry out all of Sly's commands and to inform him he has been mad and that his wife laments his sickness. Some of the attendants carry Sly off-stage.

A trumpet is heard, and the lord sends one of his men to inquire whose approach it heralds. The servant returns to inform his master that a company of travelling players has arrived. The players enter immediately, and the leader of the troupe offers their services to the lord, who requests them to act before a guest of his, by whose odd behavior they must not be disturbed. The leading actor assures him that they can contain themselves "were he the veriest antic of the world." A servant leads the players to the lord's house.

The lord then gives orders that Bartholomew, his page, be dressed as a lady so that he may pretend to be Sly's wife. He further suggests that the boy should weep (with the help of an onion in his handkerchief, if necessary), show affection for Sly and say that "she" is glad to see her husband restored to health after he has, for seven years, considered himself a beggar. A servant goes out to put these plans into action. The lord follows, eager to see the arrangements made and to make sure by his own presence that his men do not overdo the baiting of Sly.

Commentary

The scene introduces the main characters of the framework material and expounds the situation. It also introduces the players who are to perform *The Taming of the Shrew* and demonstrates the occasion of the performance.

Shakespeare is almost certainly recalling the Warwickshire in which he spent his youth when he visualizes the action as taking place somewhere near his birthplace, Stratford-upon-Avon. Sly mentions in the next scene that he comes from Burton-on-the-Heath, which is a village some 16 miles from Stratford. He also states that he drinks at the alehouse of "Marian Hacket of Wincot," a place that may be identified as any of three small villages near Stratford. One of these had a Hackett family living there during Shakespeare's lifetime and another, Wilmcote, is the place where Shakespeare's mother was born.

In his opening exchange with the hostess, Sly speaks the naturalistic prose that is to characterize his speeches in the next scene. He also makes a gesture of ludicrous pretentiousness: "The Slys are no rogues. Look in the chronicles: we came in with Richard Conqueror" (Induction 1, 3-4). This remark prepares the audience for his gradual acceptance, in the next scene, of his new position as a nobleman.

His long description of how Sly is to be treated and his detailing of the setting in which the tinker is to be placed cause the audience to see the lord as a kind of stage manager. He is going to make "a flattering dream or worthless fancy" appear to be the truth to Sly. This places him, metaphorically, in the same situation as the players, who are to do the same thing for the audience with the inset play (that is, the play which Sly witnesses).

In deciding to make an experiment in the manipulation of human personality, the lord is also a parallel to Petruchio, who is to try the same experiment with Kate. The lord perceives that Sly is a "monstrous beast" owing to the effects of drink, so he wishes to make the tinker into a gentleman simply by treating him like one. Similarly, Petruchio's technique is to treat Kate, who is "monstrous" with pride and shrewishness, as if she were gentle, thus making her so.

By profession masters of illusion, the players are fit servants for the lord, who notes among the players one who "wooed a gentlewoman so well," thus preparing the audience for the theme of the inset play. He also makes a further connection between the framework and inset play by introducing the idea of the marriage relationship through providing Sly with a wife who is no wife.

Certain image patterns are to be used in the play to reflect the main themes. Music imagery is related to the idea of harmoniousness in human relationships. Clothes imagery underscores the idea of deceptive human appearances. Imagery of material wealth is used to convey the value of human love. All of these associated images and themes make their appearance in this scene: "music . . . to make a dulcet and a heavenly sound" is designed to soothe Sly's drunken brain, "the sweet clothes" he is to be dressed in are to symbolize his changed status and the rings and silver basins are associated with the love of his page-wife.

INDUCTION 2

Summary

In a richly furnished chamber in the lord's house, Christopher Sly, dressed in nightclothes, is sleeping, surrounded by the lord and his servants, each of whom holds clothes, washing equipment or other accessories. Sly awakens and calls for a pot of ale. On being offered various lordly articles of clothing and fine foods, he stoutly asserts his identity and profession. The lord comes forward and laments that "a mighty man, of such descent/ . . . Should be infused with so foul a spirit." He answers Sly's protests that he is a tinker from Burton-on-the-Heath with the explanation that Sly has been the victim of "a strange lunacy." To support his point, the lord indicates the attendant servants, orders music to be played and describes how a beautiful bed, fine horses and the pleasures of hawking and hunting are all Sly's to command. The servants, following their master's cue, enter the conversation to describe the fine paintings Sly possesses depicting erotic subjects from classical mythology.

On perceiving that Sly is growing convinced by their talk, the lord adds:

> Thou art a lord, and nothing but a lord.
> Thou hast a lady far more beautiful
> Than any woman in this waning age.
> (Induction 2, 59-61)

Slowly, Sly is persuaded that he is not dreaming, that he is "a lord indeed,/And not a tinker nor Christophero Sly." He is assured that he has slept for many years, during which time he has called out the names of people and places of which the servants had never heard. (Here they name Sly's real acquaintances and refer to his alehouse environment.)

Bartholomew, the lord's page, enters dressed as a lady. He is accompanied by attendants, one of whom offers Sly a pot of ale. Sly is persuaded that the page is indeed his "noble lady" and at once orders the servants to retire so that his wife might go to bed with him. The page excuses himself from Sly's bed for a night or two on the grounds that the physicians

> . . . have expressly charged,

In peril to incur your former malady,
That I should yet absent me from your bed.

(Induction, 119-121)

Sly is so unwilling to fall into his former sleep that he accepts the excuse docilely enough.

A servant enters and announces to Sly that his "honor's players," hearing that he has recovered from his illness, have come to present before him a pleasant comedy, which will act as an antidote to sadness and melancholy by framing his mind "to mirth and merriment,/Which bars a thousand harms and lengthens life." Sly questions the servant about the type of entertainment that is planned and, on being assured it is a "kind of history," he bids his "wife" sit by his side and prepares to witness the performance.

Commentary

This scene develops the intentions of the lord expressed in the previous scene. It displays at length Sly's character and his gradual acceptance of his new situation. It also prepares the audience for the beginning of the play within the play by setting up various parallels between the themes of the main plot and those of the framework.

The splendidly equipped chamber in a country mansion, with its rich furnishings and erotic pictures, is in sharp contrast to the heath and low tavern of the previous scene. This setting helps to make Sly's conviction that he is a lord more credible.

Sly's gradual belief in his changed status is well managed. From the moment of awakening, when he calls for ale, and from his initial disbelief and the assertion of his identity as "old Sly's son of Burton-Heath, by birth a pedlar, by education a card-maker, by transmutation a bear-herd, and now by present profession a tinker," he finally, under the persuasion of the lord, moves to his acceptance of his new position: "Am I a lord? and have I such a lady? Or do I dream? . . . Upon my life, I am a lord indeed." After the introduction of his "wife," his comic reaction to the new manners he is forced to learn is realistically observed:

Sly: . . . What must I call her?
Lord: Madam.
Sly: Al'ce madam, or Joan madam?

Lord: "Madam" and nothing else, so lords call ladies.

. . . .

Sly: Madam, undress you and come now to bed.

The servants and the lord complement each other's appeals to Sly. For example, the servants add plausibility by their references to Sly's companions, and the lord nicely times the introduction of the information that Sly has a wife for the moment when the tinker is already half persuaded.

Playing his part as the wife skilfully, the page evades Sly's romantic advances. He parallels Kate's role in the main play, for he, too, is a wife who is no wife.

The scene is constructed stylistically on the contrast between Sly's natural, idiomatic prose and the formal blank verse of the lord and his servants, with its metaphorical descriptions and wealth of classical allusions.

The images of music and clothes, introduced in the first scene, are developed here in verbal and visual terms. Sly is newly clad at the opening of the scene; he is offered clothes indicative of his changed status. Music is seen as the sign of the harmonious mind as opposed to the "strange lunacy" which Sly supposedly suffered.

ACT I · SCENE 1

Summary

The play within the play commences with a flourish of trumpets. The scene is a public square in Padua, onto which various houses open, including those of the wealthy Baptista and Hortensio, a suitor for the hand of Baptista's daughter, Bianca. Lucentio and his manservant, Tranio, enter. In a formal introductory speech Lucentio informs the audience, through his words to Tranio, that he is the son of the great merchant, Vincentio of Pisa, who has agreed that his son should visit Padua in order to study "virtue, and that part of philosophy/ . . . that treats of happiness/By virtue specially to be achieved." Tranio, while he supports his master's intention, advises that it be pursued with a sense of proportion, so that music, poetry, rhetoric and logic are used for their proper purpose and mathematics and metaphysics are studied only when the mind is attuned to them. More importantly, he urges Lucentio not to forget the joys of love and courtship.

Just as Lucentio is wishing that his other servant, Biondello, would arrive with the luggage so that they might find accommodations, the door of Baptista's house opens and Baptista enters the square with his two daughters, Bianca and Katharina. They are followed by Bianca's two suitors, one a young man, Hortensio, and the other an old one, Gremio. Lucentio and Tranio, after hazarding a guess that this company has perhaps come to welcome them to town, withdraw to one side to watch what happens.

Baptista begs Hortensio and Gremio not to ask for Bianca's hand in marriage because, as he says:

> . . . I firmly am resolved you know.
> That is, not to bestow my youngest daughter,
> Before I have a husband for the elder.
>
> (Act I, Scene 1, 49-51)

He then ironically suggests that if either of them loves Katharina, they shall have permission to court her at their leisure. Both suitors react violently to this suggestion and make it quite plain that they wish to be defended against such she-devils. Katharina resents their remarks and describes graphically how she would

38

treat husbands like them. From their point of observation, Lucentio and Tranio comment on these exchanges. Lucentio is forcibly struck by Bianca's looks and manner, while Tranio is fascinated by Katharina, whom he takes to be "stark mad or wonderful froward."

Baptista makes much of his young daughter (causing Katharina to react with jealous displeasure) and sends Bianca indoors to entertain herself with her books and instruments. Both Gremio and Hortensio express their objections to Baptista's plans for his daughters. But the father is firm and informs them further that, as he knows Bianca "taketh most delight/from music, instruments and poetry," he intends to employ schoolmasters to instruct her. He invites them to recommend suitable candidates for the posts. Going indoors to talk further to Bianca, Baptista tells Katharina to stay behind. The girl interprets this order as a violation of her freedom and deliberately follows her father into the house, slamming the door behind her.

Left to themselves, Gremio and Hortensio agree that they will find schoolmasters for Bianca and, at Hortensio's suggestion, plot to join forces to secure a husband for Katharina. Gremio is at first dubious about the success of such a plan, but Hortensio reminds him that "there be good fellows in the world, and a man could light on them, would take her with all faults, and money enough." Gremio is finally persuaded and agrees to postpone their rivalry. The two men go off together to seek a possible husband for Katharina.

Tranio and Lucentio come forward, the servant uttering his amazement that his master should fall in love with Bianca so suddenly. Lucentio assures him that he is so deeply attracted to the girl that he wishes his servant to help him secure her for his wife. Tranio vainly attempts to discuss the implications of Baptista's decision, but Lucentio is enraptured with his own vision of Bianca, whom he compares with various beauties from classical literature. In desperation, Tranio stirs him from his trance, and they plot that Lucentio shall disguise himself as a schoolmaster to teach Bianca, while Tranio shall pretend to be the young gentleman from Pisa, keeping servants and entertaining his countrymen just as Lucentio would. They immediately exchange clothes.

Biondello, Lucentio's other servant, enters and expresses surprise at their exchange of garments. However, he is told that the reversal of identities is necessary because Lucentio's life is threatened and that he, Biondello, must treat Tranio as if he were his master. As they go out, Lucentio urges Tranio to present himself at Baptista's house as a third suitor for the hand of Bianca.

Commentary

This scene has most of the functions of an opening scene. First, it introduces all of the principal characters, except Petruchio, and displays their relationships. It reveals the situation concerning Bianca and her suitors and informs the audience of Baptista's decision about the order in which he intends his daughters to marry and its implications for Gremio, Hortensio and the newly arrived Lucentio.

Most importantly, the scene introduces Katharina, who makes a strong impact with her display of temperament. Her actions make the audience aware of the nature of the challenge that Petruchio takes up in the following scene. Bianca is contrasted favorably with her sister. Thus, the contrast between their marital fortunes is initiated.

The possibility of a romantic love affair between Lucentio and Bianca is introduced as the intrigue is planned between Tranio and his master. This scheme prepares for Lucentio's appearance as Cambio in the next scene and for his subsequent courtship of Bianca.

Lucentio is the conventional, well-bred and wealthy Elizabethan young man. His lofty good intentions to study and travel are quickly shattered within the space of a few lines by the sight of Bianca, thus making ironical Tranio's speech on the pleasures of love. Having fallen in love at first sight, Lucentio soon begins to speak in the idiom of the romantic lover.

Half companion, half servant to Lucentio, Tranio speaks in a manner that makes believable his ability later in the play to carry off the role of his master successfully.

Baptista is the representative of the older generation, which so frequently in Shakespearean comedy is seen as the barrier to young love's consummation. His interest in marriage is monetary rather than romantic and, thus, probably typical of the Elizabethan older generation. His favoritism toward his younger daughter is made very clear in his treatment of the two girls. He is as guilty in his way of insulting Katharina's pride as are Gremio and Hortensio.

In her quiet responsiveness to her father's favors, and in her obedience and conventional sweetness of nature, Bianca is seen at this point in sharp contrast to her violent and shrewish elder sister. Baptista's elder daughter makes an immediate and forceful impression, both through her own words and actions and through the unflattering comments of the other characters, particularly Gremio and Hortensio. However, the scene gives ample evidence of the reasons for her shrewishness. First, she is obviously jealous of her sister's attractiveness to men. Second, she resents her father's preference for Bianca. Third, her pride as a woman has been outraged by the treatment she has received. As a result, she reacts violently against those people she thinks have most wounded her self-esteem. When this intense reaction gets out of hand, it takes the extreme form we witness here.

Aligned by age and wealth with Baptista, Gremio is obviously a candidate for baiting the younger people. Hortensio, however, is a less clearly developed representative of the stage type to which Lucentio belongs. Hortensio is a parallel to Lucentio in his love for Bianca and in the means he takes to gain access to her. This parallel is developed in his encounter with Petruchio in the next scene.

Stylistically, the scene falls into four sections: (1) the formal blank verse of the opening exchange between Lucentio and Tranio (Act I, Scene 1, 1-47); (2) the easy-moving, more natural conversational blank verse of the Baptista-Gremio-Bianca-Katharina sequence (Act I, Scene 1, 48-104); (3) the prose conversation between Gremio and Hortensio as they plot to find Katharina a husband (Act I, Scene 1, 105-142); (4) the contrasting blank verse of Lucentio, with its courtly tone and vocabulary as he describes his love for Bianca, and the plain-style verse of Tranio as he attempts to awaken his master from his reverie.

Bianca and Katharina are contrasted by the language associated with them. The former is linked to imagery of wisdom and music. For example, after her father has rejected her suitors, she says, "My books and instruments shall be my company." As Lucentio listens to Bianca's words, he remarks to his servant, "Hark, Tranio! thou mayst hear Minerva speak." On the other hand, Katharina is associated with discord and madness. Tranio says she is "stark mad," and Gremio calls her "rough" and a "fiend of hell." She is also given both vigorous prose to speak and coarse, down-to-earth verse similar to Petruchio's: ". . . doubt not her care should be/To comb your noddle with a three-legged stool."

ACT I · SCENE 2

Summary

Petruchio and his manservant, Grumio, who have just arrived from Verona to visit Hortensio, enter the public square and approach Hortensio's door. In an exchange of comic horseplay, Petruchio orders Grumio to knock on the door: "Here, sirrah Grumio, knock I say . . . knock me here soundly." The servant takes this command to mean that he is being ordered to strike his master, which he does and gets his ears wrung by Petruchio as a result.

Hortensio comes out, greets the two men affectionately and helps them to work out their misunderstanding. He then asks Petruchio why he has come to Padua and is informed by the latter that, having come into his inheritance from his recently deceased father, he travels for experience in the hope of marrying well as soon as possible.

With his recent agreement with Gremio in mind, Hortensio seizes upon Petruchio's final words and jokingly informs his friend that, if he were not so fond of him, he would recommend him to a rich but shrewish young woman. Petruchio takes up the suggestion and says that as he comes "to wive it wealthily in Padua;/If wealthily, then happily in Padua." He does not care how unattractive and shrewish the girl is, so long as her father is wealthy. Hortensio is naturally delighted with this statement and tells Petruchio of Baptista's decision regarding the marriage of his daughters, of Katharina's renown in Padua for her scolding tongue and of his own love for Bianca.

Petruchio informs Hortensio that Baptista was a friend of his father's and expresses his eagerness to see Katharina. Grumio interrupts to assure Hortensio that his master is quite capable of dealing with any shrew. Hortensio then asks Petruchio if he would be willing to introduce him as a schoolmaster to Baptista so that he might have leisure and opportunity to court Bianca unsuspected by her father and Gremio. His friend agrees to the plan.

At this moment, Gremio enters with Lucentio, who is disguised as Cambio, a schoolmaster. Petruchio, Hortensio and Grumio withdraw to one side. Gremio carefully instructs Lucentio about the books he is to use and orders him to take every opportunity while he is teaching Bianca to influence her as much as possible in favor of Gremio as a husband.

43

Not to be outdone, Hortensio comes forward and informs his aged rival that he has a friend who will procure the services of a fine musician to instruct Bianca and that, even more important, Petruchio "will undertake to woo curst Katharina." Gremio is shocked to hear this and questions Petruchio about both his background and his knowledge of Katharina's shrewish nature. The young man scornfully dismisses the old man's doubts about his ability to resist a woman's temper. Convinced, Gremio undertakes with Hortensio to absorb the expenses of Petruchio's courtship, providing he is successful in marrying Katharina.

Just as the agreement is made, Tranio, dressed as Lucentio, enters accompanied by Biondello and asks the way to Baptista's house. He overrides the objections of Hortensio and Gremio, stating that as

> Fair Leda's daughter had a thousand wooers,
> Then well one more may fair Bianca have.
> And so she shall: Lucentio shall make one.
>
> (Act I, Scene 2, 239-241)

Petruchio grows impatient at wasting time in such discussion and makes it clear to Tranio that Baptista's daughter, who is "famous for her scolding tongue," is *his* wife-to-be. Hortensio introduces Petruchio to Tranio as the man to whom all of Bianca's suitors are indebted. Tranio, in appreciation of this fact, invites all those present to meet him in the afternoon to eat and drink at his expense.

Commentary

Having been introduced to Katharina in the previous scene, we now meet Petruchio, the other protagonist. Some time is spent characterizing him as a rash, well-defined and vigorous personality. The scene also serves to draw him into the marriage scheme defined in the previous scene, and it allows him, as a friend of Hortensio's, to be the means whereby the disguised Hortensio is introduced into Baptista's household as the musician, Licio. The scene effectively furthers the Bianca subplot by having Gremio bring on Lucentio disguised as the schoolmaster, Cambio. It also gives the audience its first glimpse of Tranio acting out the role he was asked to undertake by Lucentio in the final lines of Act I, Scene 1.

Shakespeare manages within a short time to establish Petruchio as a promising adversary for the Katharina we have seen in the previous scene. His hasty nature is demonstrated by his immediate decision to woo Katharina, before he has even seen her, and despite Hortensio's warning about her temper. The assertive and confident way in which he seizes upon an opportunity and then consciously goes several steps beyond it looks ahead to his later treatment of Katharina. Thus, when told that Katharina is shrewish, he falls into outrageous exaggeration:

> By she as foul as was Florentius' love,
> As old as Sybil, and as curst and shrewd
> As Socrates' Xantippe, or a worse,
> She moves me not. . . .
>
> (Act I, Scene 2, 67-70)

Our impressions of Petruchio's character are strengthened by the confident asides of Grumio concerning his master. When Hortensio suggests to Gremio that they pay for Petruchio's expenses, the latter replies, "And so we will, provided that he win her." Grumio mutters, "I would I were as sure of a good dinner."

Emerging in this scene as an attractive clown, Grumio makes appropriate, chorus-like comic comments on most phases of the action. At one point, he places his finger on the crux of the Bianca subplot: "See, to beguile the old folks, how the young folks lay their heads together!" (Act I, Scene 2, 135-136). He is also the butt of the physical comedy of misunderstanding at the opening of the scene.

Gremio, Bianca's elderly suitor, is seen as the "pantaloon" he is called in the First Folio edition of the play: an old man foolishly in love with a young girl and an easy dupe for the quick wit of Lucentio, whom he employs in the disguise of Cambio.

Playing his master's role to the utmost, swaggering and outtalking Bianca's other suitors, Tranio is a good example of the intriguing, quick-witted servant of classical comedy.

Hortensio has no well-defined character. He is employed here chiefly as a means of introducing Petruchio. He is depicted as the conventional love-sick young man, in which role he provides some amusement in his jealous exchange with Gremio.

Petruchio's speech immediately stands out from both the

plain and the metaphorical verse that surrounds his dialogue. It has a vigor of movement and a vitality that are lacking in the speeches of the other characters. Thus, it functions as a means of characterizing him. In his common-sense observations on the action, Grumio speaks in a prose that complements his master's. Tranio's speech is fluent to the point of being rattling, and it slightly echoes Lucentio's manner of speaking in the previous scene. It is thus appropriate to the role he is now playing.

Just as Katharina has been linked with the language of discord in the previous scene, so Petruchio uses similar terminology to assert his assurance that he will have success in wooing her:

> Think you a little din can daunt mine ears?
> Have I not in my time heard lions roar?
> Have I not heard the sea, puffed up with winds
> Rage like an angry boar chafèd with sweat?
> Have I not heard great ordnance in the field,
> And heaven's artillery thunder in the skies?
> Have I not in a pitchèd battle heard
> Loud 'larums, neighing steeds, and trumpets' clang?
> And do you tell me of a woman's tongue?
>
> (Act I, Scene 2, 196-204)

ACT II · SCENE 1

Summary

In a room in Baptista's house, Katharina stands over Bianca, whose hands she has tied. The younger girl begs her sister to untie her, saying she will do anything she is commanded, while slyly making an insulting allusion to Katharina's age. Katharina questions her about her feelings with regard to Hortensio and Gremio. At Bianca's refusal to admit love for either of them, Katharina strikes her, but is prevented from doing further harm by the entrance of Baptista, who unties his younger daughter and reprimands the elder for her vicious behavior. Bianca escapes, and Katharina follows her after making clear to her father her reasons for her jealousy of her sister: "She is your treasure, she must have a husband,/I must dance bare-foot on her wedding-day." Just at this moment, Bianca's suitors enter in various disguises. Gremio is accompanied by Lucentio, disguised as Cambio the schoolmaster; Petruchio enters with Hortensio, who is dressed as Licio the musician; and Tranio, as Lucentio, follows with a page carrying a lute and some books.

Petruchio immediately introduces himself to Baptista and expresses his interest in Katharina, which he says has been aroused by reports

> . . . of her beauty and her wit,
> Her affability and bashful modesty,
> Her wondrous qualities, and mild behavior
>
> (Act II, Scene 1, 48-50)

He then presents Hortensio as a musician capable of instructing Bianca and Katharina. Baptista welcomes Petruchio but, with some embarrassment, indicates that he does not think that Katharina is the wife for him. Petruchio takes this pronouncement as Baptista's refusal to part with his daughter.

Gremio is annoyed at Petruchio's monopoly of Baptista's attention and interrupts to introduce Lucentio as Cambio, an able scholar fit to tutor the two sisters. Baptista catches sight of Tranio standing nearby and questions him about his intentions in coming to visit him. The servant introduces himself as Lucentio and announces his desire to be considered one of Bianca's suitors, in proof of which he offers the books and lute that his page is carrying. Baptista accepts the gifts, giving the instrument to Hortensio and the books to Lucentio. He then calls for a servant to lead the two new tutors to their pupils.

Petruchio makes it quite clear that he wishes to star! wooing Katharina immediately. He makes inquiries concerning the value of her dowry. Being satisfied that it is substantial, he assures Baptista of a large financial settlement for his daughter should she be left a widow and suggests that they draw up a marriage agreement at once. Baptista, however, is reluctant to act quickly until he knows Katharina is prepared to accept Petruchio as a husband. Petruchio is airily confident as he replies:

> Why that is nothing, for I tell you, father
> I am as peremptory as she proud-minded,
> And where two raging fires meet together,
> They do consume the thing that feeds their fury.
>
> (Act II, Scene 1, 130-133)

Baptista is not convinced. Just as he is warning the confident young man to expect "unhappy words," Hortensio enters with the lute broken over his head and relates how Katharina lost her temper as he attempted to teach her and attacked him with the lute. Baptista comforts him with the promise that he shall find Bianca more agreeable. He then leads out all his guests except Petruchio, to whom he promises to send Katharina.

Left to himself, Petruchio tells the audience that his campaign will consist in totally ignoring Katharina's shrewishness by the simple device of taking all antagonistic expressions she utters to mean their opposite. Katharina enters and is at once treated to a rattling speech from Petruchio, in which he asserts that she is "plain Kate" rather than the notorious "Katharina" she claims to be and that he intends to marry her. She attempts to dismiss him. There follows a bout of verbal quibbling, during the course of which she strikes him, only to be threatened with retaliation should she do so again. She attempts to leave, but Petruchio takes her in his arms despite her struggles and, against all her protests, kisses her. He then holds her fast as she strives to free herself. He tells her that rumor, which reported her to be "rough and coy and sullen," is a liar because it is obvious that mildness, pleasantness and courtesy are her outstanding qualities. He releases her and, withstanding a further barrage of insults, informs her that he is destined to marry and tame her.

Baptista, Gremio and Tranio re-enter the room, and Petruchio announces the success of his courtship. Surprised at seeing Katharina so silent, Baptista asks her what the matter is. She angrily replies that she regards the husband her father has apparently chosen for her as "one half lunatic, / A madcap ruffian." Petruchio brushes aside these protests and assures Baptista that, in private, Katharina is really as "temperate as the morn" and as "modest as the dove." He says further that they have agreed between themselves that she shall act "curst" in company and that they wish to be married on the coming Sunday. Baptista gives his blessing to the match. Petruchio seizes Katharina in his arms and forcibly kisses her again. She rushes out of the room, and Petruchio leaves to go to Venice to buy clothes for his wedding day.

Baptista turns to Gremio and Tranio and, in keeping with his promise, now announces that Bianca is free to be married to the man who will offer her the most financial security. The two suitors argue insultingly with each other over who loves Bianca most. When Gremio gives an account of his wealth and of his rich possessions, Tranio replies by declaring himself to be his father's only heir and listing his parent's rents, lands, trading ventures and houses. Baptista weighs the two offers and, deciding that Tranio's sounds better, declares that on the Sunday following Katharina's wedding, Bianca shall be married to Tranio, providing his father supports the match and agrees to its financial terms. In the event of his not doing so, Gremio shall be Bianca's bridegroom.

Baptista leaves after making his decision. He is followed by Gremio, who tells Tranio he thinks his father would be a fool to agree to such terms. Tranio, addressing the audience, acknowledges the difficulty before him, but sees that it may be overcome: "I see no reason but supposed Lucentio / Must get a father called — supposed Vincentio."

Commentary

So far as the main plot is concerned, we are given two glimpses of Katharina and Petruchio: first, in contact with other characters and second, when they engage in their first personal duel, with its promise of Petruchio's future success. The scene also advances the subplot by showing the successful introduction of Lucentio and Hortensio (disguised respectively as Cambio and

Licio) into Baptista's household and by showing the skill of Tranio in outbidding Gremio for Bianca's hand. It also raises the difficulty of finding someone to take Vincentio's place in order to secure Baptista's agreement to the match.

The action is divided into six main sections: (1) the Bianca-Katharina exchange (Act II, Scene 1, 1-36); (2) the introduction of the disguised suitors into Baptista's house (Act II, Scene 1, 38-110); (3) Petruchio's proposal to Baptista and Hortensio's discomfiture (Act II, Scene 1, 111-168); (4) Petruchio's first statement of his policy and his first encounter with Katharina (Act II, Scene 1, 169-282); (5) the setting up of the wedding (Act II, Scene 1, 283-326); (6) the bidding for Bianca's hand (Act II, Scene 1, 327-413).

Those sections dealing with the subplot prepare the audience for later scenes. The introduction of the disguised suitors anticipates the comic wooing in Act III, Scene 2. The bidding for Bianca's hand makes it necessary for Tranio to obtain the pedant's services in Act IV, Scene 4. Petruchio's first encounter with Katharina gives the audience a taste of his campaign, which is to flower in Act IV, Scenes 1, 3 and 5. The arranging of the match looks ahead to the comic wedding in Act III, Scene 2.

This is an important scene insofar as Katherina's characterization is concerned. Her jealousy of Bianca's popularity is made clear in the opening lines, and one of the root causes of her shrewishness is displayed in her words to her father:

> She is your treasure, she must have a husband,
> I must dance bare-foot on her wedding-day
> And for your love to her lead apes in hell.
>
> (Act II, Scene 1, 32-34)

In her exchange with Petruchio, her wit and spirit emerge. Although she resists his marital intentions, it is noticeable that in Act III, Scene 2, 8-20, her concern is not that she is being forced to marry, but that Petruchio has failed to come for her as he had promised. Katharina is, in fact, able to accept Petruchio's proposal because the stance he adopts allows her to be married and yet appear to be won against her will. Thus, she can remain consistent within the attitude she has unconsciously adopted.

Although he appears decisive and reckless in desiring to marry Katharina, Petruchio's method of attack is consistent with his appearance and actions in Act I, Scene 2. He alone is able to see what is wrong with Katharina, realizing at once that the only cure lies in meeting her behavior with more of its own kind. He knows, too, that in any conflict of will with Katharina, he will emerge the victor because his "shrewishness" is consciously assumed and therefore in his control, whereas hers has developed subconsciously and is not in her control. The effectiveness of his approach is displayed in their verbal exchange, during which Katharina is continually reduced to speechlessness. It is obvious from the stage directions and from Petruchio's own utterances that he is immediately attracted by Katharina's spirit.

Exemplifying the extremely non-romantic view of matrimony in this scene, Baptista "auctions off" Bianca to the highest bidder, despite his lip service to the necessity for marital affection. He hypocritically tells Petruchio he will agree to his marrying Katharina "when the special thing is well obtained, / That is, her love; for that is all in all." (Act II, Scene 1, 128-129).

Bianca's mildness is contrasted with her sister's violence. Yet, despite the fact that she is Katharina's victim at the opening of the scene, she shows herself quite capable of verbally striking Katharina where she is most vulnerable. Note, for example, her reference to the difference in their ages in "so well I know my duty to my elders" (Act II, Scene 1, 7) and her allusion to Katharina's lack of suitors in "is it for him you do envy me so?" (Act II, Scene 1, 8).

Lucentio's servant, Tranio, builds upon our first impression of him as the quick-witted and resourceful intriguer when he out-does Gremio in bidding for Bianca's hand and plans to obtain a false father for Lucentio. Hortensio, meanwhile, begins to emerge as the losing suitor as he becomes the butt for both verbal and visual comedy at Katharina's hands.

The images of music and storm are taken up in this scene in different ways, and both are related to Katharina's behavior. Petruchio sees his relationship with Katharina in terms of violent gusts and winds. Katharina's disharmony is given graphic visual expression as Hortensio enters after she has broken the lute over his head and verbal expression as he describes the form her irritation with him took:

I did but tell her she mistook her frets

. . .
When, with a most impatient devilish spirit,
'Frets, call you these?' quoth she, 'I'll fume with them.'

(Act II, Scene 1, 149-52)

The scene also contains the first display of Katharina's and Petruchio's brilliance of tongue. Their blank verse is filled with vigorous phrases taken from everyday speech, and it is reminiscent of the language of Christopher Sly. Katharina, for example, calls Petruchio "a madcap ruffian and a swearing Jack," "a frantic fool" and "a mad-brain rudesby." Petruchio, with his verbal inventiveness, reduces her pride to ordinary proportions:

You lie, in faith, for you are called plain Kate,
And bonny Kate, and sometimes Kate the curst.
But Kate, the prettiest Kate in Christendom,
Kate of Kate-Hall, my super-dainty Kate,
For dainties are all cates and, therefore, Kate.

(Act II, Scene 1, 185-89)

ACT III · SCENE 1

Summary

In a room in Baptista's house, Hortensio, disguised as Licio, sits teaching Bianca to play the lute. Lucentio, disguised as Cambio, stands apart, waiting for his turn to teach her Latin. As Hortensio explains the fingering of the instrument, he takes Bianca's hand in his, at which point Lucentio grows indignant and reproves him, reminding him of the violent reception Katharina gave him. Hortensio, however, defends his right to teach Bianca music for one hour, after which time Lucentio is to have his opportunity. His rival, on the other hand, sees music as that which should refresh the mind after study. The two tutors begin to quarrel, only to be separated by their pupil. She points out that she is not a child in school, tied to certain times for certain lessons, and asserts she will be taught what she chooses. Her choice is clearly for Cambio's Latin rather than for Licio's music. She sends the latter aside to tune his instrument while she attends to Cambio's lecture. As the Latin lesson proceeds, Lucentio uses the pretence of interpreting two lines of Ovid as a cover to inform Bianca of his real identity, of the role that Tranio is playing and of his love for her.

Before Bianca can reply to this declaration, Hortensio interrupts with the assertion that his lute is now in tune, but after playing only one note, he is quickly sent away by Bianca to tune it again. As he steps aside, Bianca immediately takes up the Latin book and, using the same pretence as Lucentio, informs him that he should not despair, for while she cannot wholly trust him yet, she is not insensitive to his wooing. Hortensio, jealously suspecting that Cambio is courting his mistress, steals up behind them to listen to their conversation. They detect his presence, however, and carry on their exchange under the guise of discussing a point of classical mythology.

Bianca turns her attention to Hortensio, and Lucentio, now jealous in his turn, withdraws a little to watch, saying in an aside, ". . . but I be deceived/Our fine musician groweth amorous." Bianca sits next to Hortensio, who pleads with her to read his setting out of the elements of the musical scale before he teaches her the rudiments of fingering. She protests that she knows musical notation, but nevertheless reads the paper she is given. This turns out to be a declaration of Hortensio's love for her, set against the

53

basic musical notes. Just as she is making it clear to Hortensio that his lesson gives her no pleasure, a servant enters with a request from her father that she leave her lessons in order to decorate Katharina's chamber in preparation for her sister's wedding to Petruchio the following day.

Bianca bids farewell to both young men and goes out, followed quickly by Lucentio. Left to himself, Hortensio informs the audience that he believes Cambio is in love with Bianca. He vows that if he discovers she returns this affection, he will abandon his courtship of her and marry some other woman.

Commentary

This scene deals entirely with the subplot. It shows the success of Lucentio's plan to woo Bianca by making it sufficiently clear that Bianca obviously prefers him over Hortensio. It also illustrates a side of Bianca's character that has not been seen thus far and prepares the audience for the wedding of Katharina and Petruchio, which is to take place in the following scene.

The action is divided into two parallel sections: Lucentio's disguised wooing of Bianca and her favorable reception to it, followed by Hortensio's secret wooing and his lack of success. These two developments look ahead to Act IV, Scene 1, where it is quite clear that the affair between Bianca and Lucentio has progressed along the lines suggested here. Hortensio's exit lines prepare the audience for his hedging later in his pursuit of Bianca in Act IV, Scene 1:

Yet if thy thoughts, Bianca, be so humble.
To cast thy wandering eyes on every stale,
Seize thee that list — if once I find thee ranging,
Hortensio will be quit with thee by changing.

(Act III, Scene 1, 87-90)

Up to this point, our impression of Bianca has come mainly from the words of other characters (Baptista, Lucentio and Hortensio), and we have seen her contrasted favorably with her sister. Now she begins to emerge as a girl who, while outwardly obedient and sweet-tempered, is quite capable of and quite willing to carry on an amorous intrigue, even though it runs counter to her father's wishes. Her roundabout flirting with Lucentio — "I know you not . . . I trust you not . . . take heed he hear us not . . . despair not" — is a sharp contrast to Katharina's all too open and direct dealings. Hortensio's exit lines reinforce the impression of Bianca's character conveyed by the scene as a whole. Bianca also displays her self-will in the lines:

> I am no breeching scholar in the schools.
> I'll not be tied to hours nor 'pointed times,
> But learn my lessons as I please myself.
> (Act III, Scene 2, 18-20)

These are a curious echo of Katharina's words in the opening scene:

> Why, and I trust I may go too, may I not?
> What, shall I be appointed hours, as though, belike,
> I knew not what to take and what to leave?
> (Act I, Scene 1, 102-4)

Bianca's tutor in music is merely the butt for most of the humor in the scene. But, seen here as the confident lover and the intriguer with a ready tongue, Lucentio is able to turn his knowledge to an amorous end. His use of learning in this scene is very much at odds with his expressed intention of studying in Padua, which he spoke of during his first appearance. Although he is clearly the favored suitor, some suspense is maintained by his jealous watching of Hortensio.

The musical imagery, used so far to contrast the "froward" and unharmonious Katharina with the harmonious Bianca, is developed in this scene, though it is used here somewhat differently than in earlier scenes. Bianca is again called the "patroness of heavenly harmony," but as the scene progresses, she clearly prefers conversation with her "wrangling pedant" to the practice of music. Lucentio, too, is seen as the interrupter of music and is called a "base knave that jars." Hortensio is simply a musician out of tune. The whole scene is marked by quibbling references to disharmony as the three young people deceive and pretend.

ACT III · SCENE 2

Summary

In the public square in front of Baptista's house, the wedding party is awaiting the arrival of Petruchio. Gremio, Tranio (as Lucentio), Lucentio (as Cambio) and Baptista are all present, as is Katharina, dressed in her bridal array and attended by Bianca.

Baptista expresses to Tranio his concern that the bridegroom has not appeared, although everything is prepared for the wedding ceremony. Katharina claims that the shame is hers rather than her father's and she bitterly criticizes Baptista for forcing her to give her "hand opposed against [her] heart/Unto a mad-brained rudesby, full of spleen," who wooed in haste and means to wed at leisure. Tranio attempts to comfort the father and daughter by affirming Petruchio's good qualities, but Katharina merely wishes she had never set eyes on him and goes indoors weeping, followed by Bianca.

Lucentio's servant, Biondello, comes running in and announces in a roundabout way that Petruchio is approaching, dressed in disreputable clothes and riding a worn-out old horse. Petruchio is accompanied by Grumio, who is similarly attired. Baptista is amazed by the description, but is assured by Tranio that Petruchio often "goes but mean-apparelled."

At this moment, Petruchio noisily enters the square with Grumio and, being coldly greeted by Baptista, loudly demands his bride. On seeing the surprised expression on the surrounding faces, he demands to know why they are staring at him so strangely. Baptista says that his clothes are a disgrace to a solemn wedding service, but these complaints are pushed aside by Petruchio, who notes, "To me she's married, not unto my clothes." With this remark, he dashes out to find Katharina and be married. He is followed by Gremio, Grumio and Baptista.

Tranio and Lucentio, left to themselves, turn to discussing their own affairs. Tranio informs his master of his intention to find someone to pretend to be Vincentio and make the necessary promises to Baptista in order to obtain Bianca's hand in marriage. Lucentio remarks that, if it were not for Licio's watching Bianca so closely, he would marry her in secret so that neither father nor suitors could do anything when presented with an accomplished deed. Tranio promises to give some thought to assisting Lucentio in this plan.

Gremio returns from the church and reports at length what the wedding ceremony was like. He tells Tranio that Petruchio is worse than Katharina, for he swore during the service, knocked the prayer book onto the floor, struck the priest, loudly drank to the bride's health, threw wine in the sexton's face and kissed the bride with a loud, smacking noise.

The wedding procession enters, preceded by the minstrels. Petruchio offers thanks to everyone and announces that he will not stay for the wedding feast, as he intends to return to his home in the country without delay. Katharina and some of the guests beg him to stay, but while acknowledging his wife's plea, he refuses to change his mind and orders Grumio to get the horses ready. Katharina, at this point, decides that it is time to exert her will and declares she will not accompany her husband. She orders the guests to enter the house. Petruchio deliberately misunderstands her outburst and, pretending to be angry because the guests do not enter the house immediately as Katharina has commanded, attempts to drive them indoors. He then seizes Katharina around the waist and, as though in defiance of the company, acts as if he were rescuing her from them, calling on Grumio to help him. Finally, he carries Katharina bodily from the stage, with Grumio making a pretence of covering their retreat.

The members of the wedding party express their amusement and disbelief at the behavior of the "madly-mated" pair and, at Baptista's invitation, go into the house to partake of the wedding banquet. Tranio and Bianca take the places of the absent bride and groom.

Commentary

This scene illustrates the development of Petruchio's plan for Katharina's taming and the degree of its initial success. It also advances the subplot as Tranio and Lucentio plan to present a false Vincentio and contemplate the possibility of Lucentio's marrying Bianca in secret.

The action can be divided into five main sections: (1) the preparation for Petruchio's approach (Act III, Scene 2, 1-29); (2) Biondello's description of Petruchio and Petruchio's entrance (Act III, Scene 2, 30-123); (3) Tranio's and Lucentio's plotting to find a substitute Vincentio and to arrange a possible secret marriage (Act III, Scene 2, 124-143); (4) Gremio's description of the wedding (Act III, Scene 2, 144-179); (5) Petruchio's and Katharina's entrance and first marital conflict (Act III, Scene 2, 180-248).

In the public dealings between Petruchio and Katharina, the whole scene serves as a direct contrast to the secret marriage arrangements made between Bianca and Lucentio in the previous scene.

The spirited Katharina seen in Act III, Scene 1, is here ready to obey her father's wishes and is quite prepared to accept Petruchio as a husband. Her speech to the assembled company as she awaits Petruchio is not that of a shrew but that of a disappointed girl. Her inclination is not to rage but to weep. Her words clearly show that her disappointment lies in the possibility of her not being married rather than in being married against her will (see Act III, Scene 2, 8-20). This impression is reinforced by Gremio's report of her behavior during the wedding ceremony, when she "trembled and shook." It is only after the ceremony, when Petruchio's treatment reminds her of the earlier affront to her pride, that she rebels. A hint of her future obedience to Petruchio is noticeable in the line "Now, if you love me, stay."

In this scene, we also see the careful completion of the plan that Petruchio outlined in Act II, Scene 1. First, he creates a sense of disappointment; then, he qualifies the relief felt at his arrival by his eccentricity; and, finally, he counteracts Katharina's wishes by pretending to defend her from the imaginary wrongs of others. However, during his wild behavior, he is careful to point out to the guests that Katharina "is my goods, my chattels." His action in taking her forcibly from the feast is symbolic in that Katharina is not yet an agreeable housewife.

The musical motif reappears, this time ironically, as the minstrels lead in the bridal procession. The clothes motif is also developed. As Lucentio has assumed another personality and a disguise to woo Bianca, so Petruchio's dress indicates his assumption of the role of "mad-brain rudesby" to tame Kate. Biondello's long description of Petruchio's outlandish appearance has the function of fixing the point in the audience's mind. When Petruchio finally makes his entry, he himself interprets the motif for us:

To me she's married, not unto my clothes.

Could I repair what she will wear in me.
As I can change these poor accoutrements,
'Twere well for Kate and better for myself.
(Act III, Scene 2, 113-116)

This scene contains some of the best writing in the play. Both Petruchio's and Katharina's speeches have the fine vigorous rhythms and colorful vocabulary that are to be characteristic of their exchange in the central shrew-taming scenes in the next act. Gremio's report of the wedding is a good example of Shakespeare's early descriptive narrative, and Biondello's description of Petruchio's approach is delivered in rollicking prose.

ACT IV · SCENE 1

Summary

Grumio, shivering and spattered with mud, enters the hall of Petruchio's house in the country. The room has a fireplace, a table and benches, and a staircase in the rear leading to the upstairs chambers. He sits for a moment on one of the benches and complains about the journey that he, his master and new mistress have just completed. He tells the audience of the bad weather, of the poor roads and of the beatings he has received. He starts to fan the fire as he has been ordered to do and then calls for his fellow servant, Curtis.

Curtis enters and questions Grumio about the news from the city and, more particularly, about the reported shrewishness of his new mistress. Through comic misunderstanding, Grumio side-steps most of the questions he is asked and orders Curtis to stir up the fire, expressing the hope that all is in readiness for the master's coming. Curtis does as he is told and then repeats his request for news of the journey. After playfully striking him, Grumio launches into a narrative of Petruchio's outrageous behavior to Katharina and himself when their horses stumbled on the rough road.

Grumio then calls for the other servants — Nathaniel, Philip, Joseph and Nicholas — who enter in their new uniforms to greet him. Just as he is about to give them instructions concerning their reception of their master and mistress, the doors are flung open and Petruchio and Katharina enter, muddy from head to foot. Petruchio strides into the room and immediately starts abusing the servants for their lack of service. He condemns Grumio in particular for his laxness in not meeting his wife and him some way from the house as he was ordered to. Grumio endeavors to excuse himself and his fellow servants on the grounds that their new uniforms are not in perfect order. However, this excuse is swept aside by his master, who promptly orders supper to be served. Catching sight of Katharina, still standing rebelliously at the door, he pleasantly invites her to join him.

Interspersing his actions with encouraging remarks to Katharina and with snatches of songs, Petruchio then mistreats each of his servants in turn: he strikes the man who kneels to pull off his boots, deliberately upsets the water brought for him to wash in and finds fault with a dish of mutton, which he hurls at the servant who brings it. Finally, he chases them all from the room, except for Curtis. This display subdues his wife somewhat, and she criticizes him gently: "I pray you, husband, be not so disquiet, / The meat was well, if you were so contented." She is assured by her husband that it was badly burned meat, which he feels they should avoid, since it "engenders choler" and "planteth anger," and both of them are already irritable by nature. Vowing that they shall both fast that night, he leads her upstairs to the bridal chamber, followed by Curtis.

The servants creep back into the room. One of them remarks that their master appears intent on killing his wife "in her own humor." Curtis comes downstairs and informs Grumio that Petruchio is in the bedroom lecturing Katharina about the virtues of sexual restraint, while she "knows not which way to stand, to look, to speak, / And sits as one new-risen from a dream." They hear their master coming and scurry from the room.

Petruchio comes downstairs and explains his actions and future intentions to the audience. He says he means to tame Katharina as a hunter tames a falcon — that is, by keeping her without food. He announces that, during the coming night, he intends to find fault with the making of the bed in order that she shall get no sleep, pretending that all he does is "in reverend care of her." After humorously inviting anyone in the audience to tell him a better way of taming a shrew, he returns to the bridal chamber to carry out his plans.

Commentary

This scene elaborates on what has already been seen of Petruchio's shrew-taming plan in the wedding scene with Grumio's report of the journey and with the visual demonstration of Petruchio's method. Petruchio's address to the audience concerning his future plans takes up the note he struck in Act II, Scene 1, 168-180 and prepares the audience for his behavior in Act IV, Scene 3.

The scene change from Padua to Petruchio's country house is significant. Frequently in Shakespeare's plays, a change of place indicates a change in character. The country house is the locale where Katharina undergoes her reformation, so that when she next returns to Padua in Act V, Scene 1, Petruchio's victory is complete. Grumio's stress on the cold, inhospitable aspects of the scene are symbolic of Katharina's present unsuitability as a housewife and of her cold reception at her husband's hands.

During the early part of this scene, Grumio, using Curtis as a foil, develops into a quick-talking reflection of his master. His wit is displayed by his recounting of the journey while denying he will do so.

Katharina's reactions to her husband's rough behavior look forward to the moment of her final submission. Her physical ordeal on the road from Padua has subdued her completely. Only twice does she attempt to subdue Petruchio's anger, and it is noticeable that her tone is conciliatory rather than rebellious: "Patience, I pray you, 'twas a fault unwilling" and "I pray you, husband, be not so disquiet."

Petruchio's behavior is totally consistent with his original intention of wooing "not like a babe." Yet, in pursuit of his plan, he inserts reminders of Kate's unpleasant nature into his speech as he has done earlier:

> And better 'twere that both of us did fast,
> Since, of ourselves, ourselves are choleric,
> Than feed it with such over-roasted flesh.
>> (Act IV, Scene 1, 160-162)

His address to the audience describing his proposed treatment of Katharina during the night serves to build up the off-stage "taming," which adds to the effect of Act IV, Scenes 3 and 5.

The Curtis-Grumio exchange in the first part of the scene is contrasted in its vigorous colloquial prose with the highly colored, abusive verse of Petruchio's "shrewishness." Petruchio's particular manner of speaking, which is to be seen in its most extreme form in Act IV, Scene 3, is apparent here as he berates his servants, calling one of them "a whoreson, beetle-headed, flap-eared knave." (Act IV, Scene 1, 141) In his final soliloquy, the rhythm of his speech changes to a slower and smoother pace as he describes his taming method in a vivid Shakespearean metaphor derived from falconry:

> My falcon now is sharp and passing empty,
> And till she stoop, she must not be full-gorged,
> For then she never looks upon her lure.
> Another way I have to man my haggard,

To make her come and know her keeper's call:
That is, to watch her as we watch these kites
That bate and beat and will not be obedient.

(Act IV, Scene 1, 177-183)

The primary motif in the scene is that of housekeeping and hospitality, for it is in these terms that Petruchio starts to teach Katharina to be housewifely.

ACT IV · SCENE 2

Summary

In the public square in front of Baptista's house, Lucentio (as Cambio) is seated reading a book with Bianca. Hortensio (as Licio) and Tranio (as Lucentio) come out of the former's house talking together. Tranio expresses surprise that his companion should imagine that Bianca could love anyone but himself. Hortensio, however, assures him that he shall witness for himself exactly where Bianca's affections lie. He draws Tranio to one side to observe Lucentio and Bianca, who are expressing their love for each other, under the pretence of talking about the master-pupil relationship.

Hortensio questions Tranio again as to whether, in the light of the scene they are witnessing, he is still sure of possessing Bianca's affection. Tranio pretends surprise, at which Hortensio reveals his true identity. Both swear to give up their pursuit of Bianca. Before leaving the stage, Hortensio informs his companion that within three days he intends to marry a widow who has long loved him.

Tranio joins his master and Bianca, informing them of Hortensio's decision. Hortensio, he says, has gone to visit the "taming school" for shrews that Petruchio runs in the country. Biondello, who has been ordered by Tranio to watch the highway for travellers coming to Padua, enters and tells them that there is an old man, who looks like a merchant or pedant, approaching. Tranio decides to deceive the man with a false story so that the stranger will be glad to play the part of Lucentio's father and give assurance to Baptista in support of his "son's" marriage to Bianca.

The two lovers go into Baptista's house and leave Tranio to encounter the pedant, who enters at this moment. Tranio greets him and asks him the purpose of his travels, his destination and his place of origin. On being informed by the pedant that he comes from Mantua, Tranio tells him that a disagreement has developed between the rulers of Padua and Mantua concerning maritime and trade affairs, so that a sentence of death awaits any Mantuan in Padua.

Tranio takes advantage of the pedant's alarm at this news and inquires whether he has ever been in Pisa and if he knows a merchant called Vincentio. On being assured by the pedant that he has heard of Vincentio, Tranio tells him that the man is his father and suggests that he pretend to be Vincentio during his stay, lodge at Lucentio's house and "pass assurance of a dower in marriage" between Lucentio and Bianca. The pedant expresses his gratitude at the opportunity to thus escape danger and agrees to go along with the deception. They then enter Lucentio's lodgings to prepare for the coming meeting with Baptista.

Commentary

The action in this scene is divided into two sections: the alienation of Hortensio and the obtaining of the substitute Vincentio. The scene contributes to the development of the subplot by showing the audience the complete understanding now reached by Bianca and Lucentio and by eliminating Hortensio from the running for Bianca's hand. It thus prepares the audience for Act V, Scene 1, when the real Vincentio is locked out of his son's house; for Act IV, Scene 4, when Lucentio and Bianca are married secretly; and for the final scene, when the widow, whom Hortensio has married, is introduced.

The unsatisfactory nature of Hortensio's role emerges here. Apart from the scene in which he made his first appearance and apart from the courtship scene in Act III, Scene 1, Hortensio has all but disappeared from the play as an effective challenger for Bianca's hand.

In a continuation of her talk with Lucentio in Act III, Scene 1, Bianca again appropriately carries on her secret affair by means of *double entendres* (statements that carry two meanings). Her method of conversation contrasts with Katharina's direct dealing with Petruchio. The comments passed upon her character by the disappointed Hortensio at the beginning of the scene serve to modify further the earlier idealized portrait of her:

> . . . I firmly vow
> Never to woo her more, but do foreswear her,
> As one unworthy all the former favors
> That I have fondly flattered her withal.
> (Act IV, Scene 2, 28-31)

There is some slight hint of her rebellious behavior in the final scene, when she replies to Tranio's assurance that Hortensio will tame his widow: "He says so, Tranio."

Although merely a functional plot character, the pedant is made credible by means of his natural reaction to Tranio's words. He represents yet another deception necessary to bring about Lucentio and Bianca's marriage.

The verse in this scene is undistinguished. The music motif makes its appearance in Hortensio's declaration that he is no musician. The clothes motif recurs in Tranio's plan to disguise the pedant.

ACT IV · SCENE 3

Summary

In the hall of Petruchio's country house, Katharina is begging Grumio to give her some food. She tells him that she has never been accustomed to beg for anything and that now she is "giddy for lack of sleep" and starved for want of meat. What she finds hardest to bear is that her husband treats her thus "under the name of perfect love." Grumio torments his mistress by questioning her about various possible dishes she might like and then refusing to give her any. At this, she violently drives him away from her.

Petruchio enters, accompanied by Hortensio, carrying a dish of meat he has prepared himself. He sets it in front of Katharina. First, Petruchio compels her to thank him for his trouble; then, he secretly encourages Hortensio to eat as much as possible; and finally, while her attention is momentarily distracted by his expressed intention of going finely dressed to Bianca's wedding, he signals Grumio to take away the plate.

Petruchio calls in a tailor and a haberdasher to show him the gown and cap prepared for Katharina. When they display the clothes, he seizes the cap, finds fault with it and throws it aside. At Katharina's angry remark that she will have the cap because "gentlewomen wear such caps as these," he merely notes that she shall have one too — when she is gentle and not before. Katharina attempts to assert herself further, but her husband deliberately misunderstands her words to mean that she agrees with his poor opinion of the hat.

Petruchio then turns his attention to the gown the tailor has brought, finding everything about it ugly. Despite the tailor's protest that it is made according to the specifications given, Petruchio says it will not do. Katharina declares she likes the gown and will have it. Petruchio now turns on the tailor and gives him a tongue-lashing in supposed defence of his wife's appearance. The tailor, however, it not to be put down, and he again asserts that the dress was made in accordance with the directions given him by Grumio, who comically proves that not one item of the instructions has been carried out. Petruchio returns the gown to the tailor and dismisses him, whispering in an aside to Hortensio that he should see that the man is well paid for his trouble.

67

Petruchio tells Katharina that they shall go to her father's house dressed in the clothes they are wearing. He lectures her on the insignificance of outward appearance compared with inner worth, concluding:

> . . . 'tis the mind that makes the body rich;
> And as the sun breaks through the darkest clouds
> So honor peereth in the meanest habit.
>
> (Act IV, Scene 3, 169-171)

He calls for the horses to be made ready, and declares that, as the time is now seven o'clock, they should reach Baptista's house by dinnertime (that is, by around midday). Katharina corrects him, noting that the time is two o'clock, not seven, and that it will be suppertime before they arrive in Padua. Petruchio promptly takes this to be a wilful display of contrariness on his wife's part, cancels the order for the horses, and says he will not go at all unless Katharina agrees with everything he says: "I will not go to-day, and ere I do, / It shall be what o'clock I say it is."

Commentary

This scene, the climax of the main plot, demonstrates the final steps in Petruchio's successful taming of his wife. The audience witnesses the actual carrying out of Petruchio's plans, which he outlined in his soliloquy at the end of Act IV, Scene 1. The scene has three major sections: (1) Grumio's keeping Katharina hungry; and Petruchio's support of his servant, under the guise of apparent concern; (2) the physical and metaphorical display of assumed false appearances; (3) the driving home of the lesson and the preparation for the journey back to Padua.

At the opening of the scene, Katharina is reduced to a state of desperation. She who "never knew how to entreat, / Nor never needed that [she] should entreat" is now forced to beg a servant for help. Thereafter, the steps of her submission are gradually charted. We witness the complete change in her: (1) she is forced by hunger to go along wih her husband's wishes; (2) her final act of defiance over the cap and gown is proved useless and brings her only a reminder that she is not "gentle;" (3) her last utterance of a simple truth is taken as an act of defiance, and she is obliged to agree with a falsehood. In short, during the scene she becomes aware, for the first time in her life, of the necessity of compromise in relations with other people.

68

Petruchio's actions are totally consistent with his intention of tormenting Katharina "under the name of perfect love." Here, again, he is careful to point out at each stage of his treatment the moral behind it. He makes it quite clear to the audience that what he is trying to do is to make Katharina abandon the false exterior she has assumed and realize that " 'tis the mind that makes the body rich."

Showing himself every bit the quick-witted servant in this scene, Grumio is particularly agile in his verbal fooling with the tailor. This exchange is functional, however, in that it complements his master's lesson to Katharina.

The unsatisfactory nature of Hortensio's role is again underscored. There is no apparent reason why he should be present in this scene. He says very little and is noticed by Petruchio only when he seeks help in depriving Katharina of meat and, later, when he wishes to pay the tailor for his trouble.

The vigorous, earthy style and vocabulary, which have characterized Petruchio and Katharina's exchanges since their first appearance, reach a high point in this scene. Petruchio, in particular, takes language to the limits of sound and sense:

> Why, this was moulded on a porringer:
> A velvet dish. Fie, fie! 'Tis lewd and filthy.
> Why 'tis a cockle or a walnut-shell,
> A knack, a toy, a trick, a baby's cap
>
> . . .
> . . . what masquing-stuff is here?
> What's this, a sleeve? 'Tis like a demi-cannon.
> What! Up and down, carved like an apple tart?
> Here's snip and nip and cut and slish and slash,
> Like to a censer in a barber's shop.
>   (Act IV, Scene 3, 64-67, 87-91)

The extravagant inventiveness of his imagination is apparent as he piles up object on object. Grumio, in his exchange with the tailor, is a sort of prose-speaking equivalent of his master. He seizes on each phrase and turns it by pun and quibble into aggressive misunderstanding.

The stately movement of Petruchio's famous final speech is in striking contrast with his earlier verbal fireworks. It develops at length the clothing motif, which has been noticed throughout the earlier scenes, and to which the cap and gown have given visual emphasis. It also prepares the audience for Katharina's symbolic act in the last scene, when she throws her cap under her foot.

ACT IV · SCENE 4

Summary
    Tranio, still acting the part of Lucentio, enters with the ped-
ant, who is dressed for his role as Vincentio. As they approach
Baptista's house, Tranio makes quite sure that his companion is
fully prepared to go through with the pretence of being
Lucentio's father. The pedant assures him that he is and recalls
that he once met Vincentio some 20 years earlier. Biondello
enters and informs Tranio that he has told Baptista of the arrival
of Lucentio's father in Padua.
    The door of the house opens and Baptista appears, followed
by Lucentio, disguised as Cambio. Tranio greets Baptista and introduces the pedant as his father. The pedant assures Baptista
that his "son" has told him of his love for Bianca and that he is
content that they should be married if Baptista is also agreeable.
Baptista, in his turn, says he is sure that Bianca loves
"Lucentio," and that he is willing to agree to the marriage, providing the pedant will act like a father to his son and assure Bianca of a satisfactory dowry.
    Baptista suggests to Tranio that the agreement between them
be drawn up in the suitor's lodging rather than in his own house
in order to avoid possible interruption by Gremio. Tranio agrees
to this and, giving a secret sign to Lucentio, asks Baptista to send
Cambio for Bianca while he sends Biondello for a clerk to draw
up the deed. Baptista does so, and Lucentio and Biondello
withdraw to one side of the stage out of sight of the others who
enter Lucentio's house.
    Left to themselves, Lucentio and Biondello come forward.
The servant comically "interprets" for Lucentio the signs made
to them by Tranio. He tells his master that, as Baptista is safely
out of the way talking to the false Lucentio and the false Vincentio, and, as there is an old priest available at nearby St. Luke's
Church, it is Lucentio's own fault if he does not marry Bianca
immediately. He then rushes out to ask the priest to prepare for
the wedding.
    Lucentio decides he will take advantage of the opportunity
offered and leaves with the intention of persuading Bianca to
marry him in secret.

Commentary

This scene brings the complications of the subplot toward their final solution by developing further the deceptions thrust upon Lucentio by his initial decision to win Bianca's hand through intrigue. The additional complication introduced by the pedant serves to make the denouement in Act V, Scene 1 more surprising.

The frequent stooping to deception in the subplot noticeably spreads to include Baptista in this scene. Himself the object of the principal deception, he now asks to have the meeting at Lucentio's house in order to deceive Gremio. Bianca's offstage deception in persuading her father that she loves Tranio is alluded to in Baptista's words: "She loveth him or both dissemble their affections."

The servant's behavior in the last part of the scene has caused some comment, for it is noticeable that he calls Lucentio "Cambio" and, in general, treats him with little respect. It is possible that Shakespeare is here suggesting that Lucentio's disguise has, in effect, put him on an equal footing with his own servant.

The verse is undistinguished in this scene. It is worth noting that verse is used in the exchange between Tranio, Baptista and the pedant as they conclude the formal arrangements of the marriage. Prose is used for the plotting between Biondello and Lucentio.

ACT IV · SCENE 5

Summary

Petruchio, Katharina, Hortensio and the servants are resting on the highway leading to Padua. Petruchio rises and orders his company to continue. He gazes at the sun and remarks: "Good Lord, how bright and goodly shines the moon!" Katharina immediately contradicts him, assuring him that he is mistaken. At this he informs her that, if she continues to cross him, he intends to turn back to his own house. Hortensio begs Katharina to say exactly what her husband wishes so that they may continue on their journey. She sees the wisdom of his advice and mockingly agrees that the sun, the moon or whatever else Petruchio wishes to call it is indeed shining.

They are about to set off again after Katharina's submission, when Petruchio catches sight of the real Vincentio coming up behind them on the road. He addresses the old man as if he were a young girl and invites his wife to embrace the "fair lovely maid." Katharina, true to her earlier promise, straightaway greets Vincentio as a "young, budding virgin, fair and fresh and sweet," only to be told by Petruchio that she must be mad not to be able to see that it is an old man she is talking to. She agrees with her husband and apologizes to Vincentio for her "mad mistaking."

Petruchio asks Vincentio where he is going and who he is. Vincentio first expresses his amazement at their eccentric behavior and then informs them that he is going to Padua to visit his son, Lucentio. On hearing the name, Petruchio tells him that they all know his son and they are at that moment on their way to attend his coming marriage to Katharina's sister, Bianca. Vincentio is unable to believe his ears at this news, but Hortensio assures him it is true.

As they all move on toward Padua, Hortensio, in an aside to the audience, suggests that he has learned from Petruchio's treatment of Katharina how to deal with the widow he intends to marry, should she prove "froward."

Commentary

The first half of the scene takes up where Act IV, Scene 3 left off and displays further the success of Petruchio in taming Katharina. The second half serves to introduce Vincentio, who is to hasten the outcome of the subplot by exposing the deception of Lucentio and Bianca and by piercing the disguises of Tranio and the pedant. The scene also serves to bring the two plots together after they have run parallel for several scenes.

The action takes place on the road to Padua. For the changed Katharina, who is returning to the scene of her former shrewishness, the journey is symbolic of the "journey" of personality that she has undergone.

The formerly shrewish Katharina shows a distinct character change in this scene. For the first time, we see her consciously humoring her husband rather than defying him, a gesture indicative of the extent to which she has been humbled. She knows that Petruchio is behaving irrationally, and her words make it clear, both to him and to the audience, that she is aware of this. For example, her address to Vincentio, in which she treats him as if he were a young girl, humorously exaggerates Petruchio's own address to him. In complying with her husband's wishes, she subtly calls him a lunatic:

> Then, God be blessed, it is the blessed sun,
> But sun it is not when you say it is not,
> And the moon changes even as your mind.
> (Act IV, Scene 5, 18-20)

She outdoes Petruchio for the first time — but it is on his own terms.

Again, Hortensio has little relevance to the scene. He is used simply to provide an accurate choric comment — "Petruchio, go thy ways, the field is won" — and to serve as a sane witness capable of convincing Vincentio of his son's approaching marriage.

The introduction of Lucentio's father serves chiefly as a plot device, for Vincentio represents the truth against which the deceit of Lucentio and Bianca is to be revealed. By travelling to Padua with Petruchio and Katharina, he is linked with the true rather than the false.

Petruchio's and Katharina's mock flattery of Vincentio is a parody of the verse spoken by Lucentio in the first scene of the play. The image used by Petruchio to express his satisfaction with Katharina's actions conveys accurately the way in which he sees their new relationship as a natural one: "thus the bowl should run,/And not unluckily against the bias." (Act IV, Scene 5, 24-25).

ACT V · SCENE 1

Summary

In the square before the houses of Lucentio and Baptista, Gremio is seated to one side dozing. The door of Baptista's house opens quietly and Biondello comes out, followed by Lucentio, who is dressed in his own clothes, and by Bianca, who is disguised. Biondello whispers to his master that the priest is waiting for them and, despite Lucentio's objections that he will be missed in the house, leads the couple off to be married.

Gremio rouses himself as they go out behind him and expresses his surprise that Cambio has not come to meet him. Petruchio, Katharina, Grumio and Vincentio enter the square at this moment and approach Lucentio's house, which Petruchio points out to Vincentio as his son's lodgings. Vincentio prevents Katharina and Petruchio from immediately proceeding to Baptista's house by inviting them to take a drink with him and his son before they go.

When he knocks on the door, Vincentio is told by Gremio that the people within are busy and that he must knock harder if they are to hear him. He knocks again and the pedant looks through the window over the door to ask the identity of the caller. Carrying off his pretence of being Lucentio's father, the pedant assures Petruchio and Katharina that Vincentio is lying about his relationship to Lucentio. He calls for an officer to arrest the old man on the grounds that he obviously means "to cozen somebody in this city under my countenance."

When Biondello returns from seeing Lucentio and Bianca safely married, he sees Vincentio and realizes that they "are all undone and brought to nothing." Nevertheless, he decides to face his old master. Therefore, he asserts that the pedant, who is still gazing out of the window, is Lucentio's father. Vincentio loses his temper at this and starts to beat Biondello, while the pedant withdraws, calling for help. Petruchio and Katharina stand aside and watch the ensuing action.

The door of the house is flung open and Tranio appears, followed by Baptista, the pedant and some servants. Tranio at once reproves Vincentio, who, in amazement at seeing his son's fine clothes on Tranio, loses his grip on Biondello, allowing him to escape. As Tranio, with Bapista's and the pedant's backing, continues to assert his identity as Lucentio against all Vincentio's facts about his humble birth, the fearful father begins to believe that Tranio has murdered his son. An officer is called for and, just as Vincentio is being led off to jail, Gremio warns Baptista that he suspects they may all be the victims of trickery as Vincentio alleges.

Biondello returns with Lucentio and Bianca. Despite his servant's pleas that he not acknowledge his father, Lucentio kneels at Vincentio's feet and begs for his forgiveness. Bianca also kneels before Baptista. The newly married pair tell their parents of Lucentio's disguise as Cambio, of Tranio's action in taking his master's part and of their secret marriage. Both Vincentio, who is still smarting under his treatment by Tranio, and Baptista are enraged by their children's deceit and storm into their respective houses to get to the bottom of the whole affair. Lucentio comforts Bianca with the promise that her father will not persist in his displeasure. They follow Baptista into the house. Gremio does likewise, taking comfort for his loss of Bianca in the likelihood of a good meal.

Petruchio and Katharina come forward from their point of observation. Katharina asks her husband to accompany her into her father's house to see "the end of this ado." Perversely, he refuses to enter unless she kisses him first. She hesitates to do so in the open street, but, when he expresses his determination to return to his own home unless she shows that she is not ashamed of him by doing as he asks, Katharina kisses him. Petruchio realizes the completeness of his victory, and they affectionately enter the house together.

Commentary

This scene provides the working out of the complications of the subplot. It ends with the achieved marriage of Lucentio and Bianca and the promise of a possible reconciliation between the parents and children. However, it is noticeable that a slight reversal is introduced immediately before the denouement, as the pedant, Biondello and Tranio persevere in their deceptions despite Vincentio's claims. The scene also postpones Vincentio's dilemma to the very last moment and thematically juxtaposes the two plots by contrasting the complete understanding and present harmony of Petruchio and Katharina's relationship with the discord created by Lucentio's and Bianca's marriage.

The scene, with its opening of the two lovers stealing secretly from the house to be married, its threats of jailing and its physical beatings, brings together verbally and visually the discordant elements present in the subplot from the beginning of the intrigue. These elements of discord, although comically resolved, do modify the audience's response to Lucentio and Bianca's romance.

A measure of how far Petruchio and Katharina's relationship has progressed is provided by the way in which they, who in Act I, Scene 1 and Act III, Scene 2 were a spectacle for others, are now the observers of the "ado" created by the very people who previously considered them to be "monstrous." Petruchio's final test of Katharina here is not simply any test, but rather the test of her affection for him — a kiss, which indicates in public that she is not ashamed of him.

Although Vincentio is a late arrival in the play, Shakespeare skilfully makes the variety of emotions he experiences in this scene credible: outrage, assertion, physical expression of his frustration, anxiety about his son's irresponsibility, fear for his son's safety and desire for revenge on Tranio in his relief at seeing his son safe and sound.

ACT V · SCENE 2

Summary

A banquet is laid out by Tranio and the servants in a room in Lucentio's house. All of the principal characters are present: Baptista and Vincentio, Gremio and the pedant, Lucentio and Bianca, Petruchio and Katharina, and Hortensio and the widow he has just married. Lucentio welcomes his guests and invites them to eat. As they do so, Hortensio indirectly refers to Katharina's shrewishness and to Petruchio's misfortune in being married to her. Petruchio deliberately misunderstands the remark and supposes that Hortensio is afraid of his widow. Coming to her new husband's aid, the widow accuses Petruchio of attributing his own marital trouble to everyone else. When Katharina demands to know exactly what she meant by her reference to Petruchio, the widow replies, "Your husband, being troubled with a shrew,/Measures my husband's sorrow by his own." Gremio and Baptista comment on the witty exchanges of the younger people, only to be interrupted by Bianca with a jest about her woe. Petruchio expresses his intention to swap a "bitter jest or two" with her, but she interrupts him by excusing herself and withdrawing from the room. She is followed by Katharina and the widow.

Turning his wit on Tranio, Petruchio refers to his role as Lucentio when he appeared to aim at Bianca's hand himself but only caught her for his master. In reply, Tranio alludes to Katharina's shrewishness, a topic that the other characters take up with enthusiasm. However, Petruchio is unconcerned about their barbed comments and suggests a wager:

> Let's each one send unto his wife,
> And he whose wife is most obedient,
> To come at first when he doth send for her,
> Shall win the wager which we will propose.
>
> (Act V, Scene 2, 66-69)

They set the stake, at Petruchio's insistence, at 100 crowns, and Lucentio immediately sends Biondello to ask Bianca to come to him. They boy returns to inform his master that she is busy and cannot come, an answer that arouses Petruchio's scorn. In his turn, Hortensio sends Biondello to ask his wife to come to him.

Again the servant returns to inform the company that the widow, suspecting the men have some jest in hand, refuses to come.

Petruchio turns to Grumio and says, "Sirrah Grumio, go to your mistress; Say, I command her come to me." Katharina appears in the doorway, to the surprise of the whole company, and Petruchio orders her to bring her sister and the widow into the room — by force, if necessary. While she goes out to fulfil the command, Baptista awards Petruchio the wager, but the latter says he will show them further proof of his wife's "new-built virtue and obedience."

As Katharina returns, dragging in the other two wives, her husband orders her to throw her cap underfoot, which she does, much to the disgust of Bianca and the widow. Lucentio tells his wife that her disobedience has cost him 100 crowns, but he is merely told by her that he is a fool for relying on her obedience.

Petruchio then orders Katharina to "tell these headstrong women / What duty they do owe their lords and husbands." She does so eloquently, pointing out that when a woman looks angrily at her husband, she is like "a fountain troubled, / Muddy, ill-seeming, thick, bereft of beauty." She then paints a picture of the marriage relationship as one in which the husband is to provide for the maintenance of his wife, whose duty it is to reward his pains with "love, fair looks, and true obedience." In her words, the rebellious wife is seen as a subject rebellious to his king. She turns her scorn on the other two women and admits that, although she was once "froward" as they are now, she has learned by experience that it is useless "to bandy word for word and frown for frown." She admits her former weakness and is now prepared, if Petruchio so wishes it, to place her hand beneath his foot.

Petruchio, however, wants no such sign of obedience and merely begs her to kiss him before leading her off to bed. Lucentio and Hortensio grudgingly admit Petruchio's victory and, together with the other characters, retire for the night.

Commentary

The scene draws together the two plots, both physically and thematically, and provides Petruchio and Katharina with their first opportunity for a public exhibition of their newly established relationship. It also dramatically points to the contrast that has been built up during the whole play between the two marriages, illustrating the way in which the original values associated with them have been inverted.

The feast is both the celebration of the weddings and the traditional stage symbol of harmony and peace, suggested in Lucentio's opening speech of welcome to his guests:

> At last, though long, our jarring notes agree,
> And time it is when raging war is done,
> To smile at 'scapes and perils overblown.
>
> (Act V, Scene 2, 1-3)

The banquet, however, becomes the setting for a further "war" between the three couples, one from which Katharina and Petruchio emerge triumphant. In fact, Lucentio's metaphors take up the very terms in which their former arguments have been conveyed.

Petruchio is completely confident in his early exchanges with the other married couples. It is quite clear by the end of the scene that Katharina has conquered him as much as he has her.

In the early part of the scene, Katharina is noticeably defending Petruchio rather than herself. It has been suggested that her final speech is either ironical or an indication that she has been completely crushed. However, there is no justification for the former supposition in the lines as they stand, and her spirit is not broken. What she is really pleading for is mutual tolerance and a "natural" relationship, in which the husband takes responsibility for his wife and her maintenance, and she offers him in return "love, fair looks, and true obedience." Her stamping on her cap may appear a "foolish duty" to the widow, but for the audience it becomes, in the context provided by the interview with the tailor and haberdasher in Act IV, Scene 3, a symbolic gesture of her rejection of her former "false appearance." Just how successful she is in her appeal is indicated by Petruchio's final words.

Lucentio and Bianca provide hints in this scene of future strife in their marriage. They are thus aligned with Hortensio and his widow. Lucentio has already been rudely awakened from his romantic dream when he comments on Bianca's lack of obedience, which has cost him "a hundred crowns since supper time," and she herself notes his foolishness in relying on her duty. It is Lucentio, too, who applies to his wife the terminology

80

formerly reserved for Katharina: it is "a harsh hearing when women are froward." Hortensio's timid behavior and the widow's obvious control of him are an ironical comment on his words concerning Katharina in the opening scene of the play: "From all such devils, good Lord deliver us."

The pace changes from the rapid one-line or two-line exchanges in the early part of the scene to the steady, dignified measure of Katharina's final eloquent appeal. This famous speech brings together many of the images used in connection with the marital relationship throughout the play: storm and calm, housewifery, strife, entertainment and clothes.

Character Sketches

Christopher Sly

Sly is a man of plain tastes: he prefers ale to sack (a strong sherry or wine). Although he claims that his family "came in with Richard Conqueror," he is slow to believe that he is truly of noble birth. When he is at last convinced that he is a lord, he does so in the spirit of one who does not understand his position but can nonetheless enjoy it while it lasts, rather than as a man completely duped. His speech is colorful and spiced with comical phrases: "Go by, Jeronimy!" and "I'll pheese you, in faith." Blustering his way through such widely varying situations as his ejection from the alehouse and his awakening in noble surroundings, he is an appealing character. Shakespeare's characterization of Sly is so well-achieved that the reader feels he knows the tinker better than he knows Lucentio, although Sly appears extensively in only one scene.

Katharina

She is called a shrew, even by her father, but Katharina has a deeper character than the title would imply. She is continually placed second in her father's affections. Bianca, the favorite, plays the long-suffering angel, increasing Baptista's distinction between the two. Katharina recognizes her sister's strategy and reacts as one can imagine she has been reacting for years. She is hurt and she seeks revenge. It is an immature response, but the only one she knows, and it serves the dual purpose of cloaking her hurt while it revenges it. The transformation which she undergoes near the end of the play is not one of character, but one of attitude. She alters dramatically from the bitter and contemptible shrew to the obedient and happy wife when she discovers that her husband loves her enough to attempt to change her for her own good, as well as for his. She learns to respond with reason and love to a husband who cares to help her, in contrast to her former striking out at those who treated her badly. Her negative attitude becomes a positive one. The shrew is not a shrew at all beneath the surface.

Petruchio

Like Katharina, Petruchio's character has two levels. On the surface, he appears to be a rough, noisy, unfeeling opportunist, one who cares nothing for Katharina's feelings so long as she has money. The careful reader, however, will find a second and truer level upon examining Petruchio's motives. Although her money is important, Katharina's real attraction is the challenge of capturing her. She has a fiery disposition and a reputation for reacting violently to people.

During and after their marriage, Petruchio's behavior seems rough and unreasonable. He is late to the wedding, drags his wife away immediately afterward, starves her and keeps her from sleeping. He offers her lovely clothes only to whisk them away. He then forces her to call the sun the moon. Closer reading reveals his reasons for these actions and proves him to be a man of intelligence, understanding and patience. He acts the madman lovingly for the sake of his wife. Certainly he is somewhat less than gentle, but he is just what Katharina needs. He maintains a keen sense of humor throughout.

Bianca
Apparently gentle in her behavior, she is gradually revealed to be an unkind sister and a disobedient wife. She fosters her father's attitude of favoritism for herself and dislike for Katharina by playing the part of a noble victim. Her disregard for Lucentio's wishes as a newlywed leads to grim speculation as to what her behavior may be when they have been married longer. Ironically, as the play ends, she is more of a shrew than her sister. Although she has a keen mind, Bianca lacks Katharina's wit and vivacity. Bianca, therefore, proves less interesting, both in her obedience and in her shrewishness, than Katharina.

Lucentio
He is a somewhat colorless suitor, devoted to Bianca for obscure reasons. Like the other characters of the subplot, he is bland and of little interest except for the part he plays in the intricate deceptions of the subplot. Both he and Bianca are rather selfish in their love. Bianca laughs at Gremio behind his back, is unsympathetic to her sister's grief and calls Katharina mad and madly mated; Lucentio deceives his future father-in-law without any qualms, and the two ignore Hortensio completely. They are perhaps a typical pair of immature lovers who think only of themselves. Yet each considers his individual wishes before those of his beloved. Lucentio scolds his wife for losing him 100 crowns, and she retorts that he should not have wagered on her obedience.

Baptista

He is the harried father who has difficulty marrying his two daughters because the older one is a notorious shrew. He is not, however, an object of sympathy, since Katharina is a shrew chiefly because of his treatment of her. He ignores the question of his daughters' happiness in seeking mates for them. He wishes, in the case of Bianca, to make a good bargain and attain the highest possible financial concessions from the suitors and, in Katharina's case, simply to be rid of a problem child. He practically auctions off his favorite, offering her to whichever suitor will give the highest dowry, without consulting her as to any preference she may have. He will give Katharina to anyone who will take her off his hands.

Vincentio

Lucentio's father is of a different mould. He is extremely fond of his son and is grief-stricken when he discovers that Lucentio may have come to harm. His temper, however, can be extreme. He displays loud anger and a desire for revenge when he learns how Tranio has tricked him.

Hortensio

He is basically a good man, but perhaps a bit foolish. He shows himself to be an honest friend to Petruchio, to whom he frankly reveals Katharina's reputation. He continues his pursuit of Bianca without encouragement from her, but finally declares that "Kindness in women, not their beauteous looks, / Shall win my love" (Act IV, Scene 2, 41-42). He is portrayed as a colorless character, lacking both individuality and originality.

Gremio

He is called a pantaloon (a clown) and is characterized as one. An elderly gentleman, he seeks the hand of a young girl, who belittles him behind his back. He is a stock character whose type was common in Italian intrigue comedy.

Grumio

Petruchio's servant is a comic character who provides several humorous scenes. He is rather dense, as is evident in his literal interpretation of Petruchio's "knock me here soundly." Yet, he is not stupid, for in other scenes his humor is not that of a fool laughed at by the audience, but of one who cracks a clever joke deliberately.

84

Tranio

He originally adopts Lucentio's position with some show of reluctance, but he displays increasing enthusiasm for the role as the play progresses, until at last he denounces Vincentio as a fake and noisily calls for the law. His light-hearted enjoyment of his part is obvious. He is a mischievous rogue.

The Widow

She is another stock character whose conduct and attitudes might have been derived from Elizabethan courtesy books. Her object is to marry an attractive young man whom she can master. The courtesy books advised eligible men against such a match with a wealthy widow who would, because of her money, eventually dominate the relationship and, because of her past marriage, inevitably compare her present husband with her first one.

Setting

Like several other Shakespeare plays, the setting of *The Taming of the Shrew* is Italy. The time and customs are approximately those of Shakespeare's own era. The duration of the drama is a week or ten days. There is an interval of a day or two between Act II and III, while Petruchio goes to Venice for "rings and things and fine array" and while Lucentio makes progress with his wooing of Bianca. There is also a short break between Acts III and IV to allow for travel to Petruchio's country house. The final scene probably takes place a week after the wedding. In true Shakespearean fashion, the scene shifts from city to country and back to city. The classical unities of time, place and action, revived by a later generation of playwrights, were at this time ignored.

Although Padua, an Italian city, is supposedly the scene of *The Taming of the Shrew*, the characters and background are English. Actual names of people living in Warwickshire at the time are given. Articles used and customs mentioned are of England, not Italy. Even the speech of the servants and Sly reflects that of the Stratford area in the sixteenth century. Fashions satirized are those worn by English ladies of the time. The Pegasus (Inn), mentioned in Act IV, Scene 4, is in London's Middle Temple.

The reader or viewer loses sight of this mixed background, however, and is conscious only of the animation and action of this situation comedy as it unrolls before him.

Image Patterns

During the present century, Shakespeare scholars have discovered that many leading ideas and themes in the plays are often conveyed by interwoven groups of verbal and visual poetic images. In *The Taming of the Shrew,* a number of these patterns or chains of imagery occur, not densely as in a play like *Macbeth,* but occasionally. Nevertheless, they are handled in a typically Shakespearean manner, and an awareness of them provides a greater understanding of the play as a whole.

Music and Harmony

Images of music and harmony are often used by Shakespeare to express metaphorically political, social and personal stability, while their opposites, discord and disharmony, are used to express an unnatural upheaval in these spheres of life.

Thus, Katharina's shrewishness is linked with musical discord, most strikingly in the passage describing Hortensio's (Licio's) attempt to teach her to play the lute:

Bap: What, will my daughter prove a good musician?
Hor: I think she'll sooner prove a soldier.
　　Iron may hold with her, but never lutes.
Bap: Why, then thou cans't not break her to the lute?
Hor: Why, no, for she hath broke the lute to me.
　　I did but tell her she mistook her frets
　　And bowed her hand to teach her fingering,
　　When, with a most impatient devilish spirit,
　　'Frets, call you these?' quoth she,
　　　'I'll fume with them'.
　　And, with that word, she struck me on the head,
　　And through the instrument my pate made way;
　　And there I stood amazed for a while,
　　As on a pillory, looking through the lute,
　　While she did call me rascal, fiddler,
　　And twangling Jack, with twenty such vile terms,
　　As had she studied to misuse me so.
　　　　　　　　　　　　(Act II, Scene 1, 144-59)

There are also many less extended musical references to Katharina's behavior throughout the play, such as the allusions to her "alarums" and those contained in her first interview with Petruchio (see Act II, Scene 1, 203-8). Conversely, Bianca's initially gentle demeanor is linked verbally with musical harmony. When she makes her first appearance, she says, "My books and instruments shall be my company, / On them to look and practise by myself" (Act I, Scene 1, 82-83). Later, Hortensio is to say of her, "this is / The patroness of heavenly harmony" (Act III, Scene 1, 4-5).

However, the pattern is not so simple as these connections would suggest, for during the course of the play we are given hints that Bianca's "harmony" is superficial, as when she rejects lute playing in favor of leisure (see Act III, Scene 1, 22-47). At the end of the play, too, after Katharina has demonstrated her "harmoniousness," it is Lucentio who remarks, in regard to his wife's defiance of his wishes, that it is "a harsh hearing when women are froward."

In the framework material, music is employed in a somewhat similar manner when it is used by the lord and his servants as a contrast to Christopher Sly's disharmonious drunkenness.

Closely linked with the musical imagery is that of uproar and tempest. This is most marked in Petruchio's speeches as he contrasts Katharina's discord with the natural and man-made discords to which he has been accustomed:

> Think you a little din can daunt mine ears?
> Have I not in my time heard lions roar?
> Have I not heard the sea, puffed up with winds,
> Rage like an angry boar chafed with sweat?
> Have I not heard great ordnance in the field,
> And heaven's artillery thunder in the skies?
> Have I not in pitched battle heard
> Loud 'larums, neighing steeds, and trumpets' clang?
> And do you tell me of a woman's tongue . . . ?
> (Act I, Scene 2, 196-204)

Love and Wealth

In Shakespeare's plays, love and wealth are frequently seen in terms of each other. Both Bianca and Katharina are looked upon by their suitors as "treasures." Petruchio comically combines the two associated images on his first appearance: "I come to wive it wealthily in Padua; / If wealthily, then happily in

Padua.'' (Act I, Scene 2, 73-74) Later, Hortensio makes the same connection in more serious terms:

> Tarry, Petruchio, I must go with thee,
> For in Baptista's keep my treasure is.
> He hath the jewel of my life in hold,
> His youngest daughter, beautiful Bianca.
>
> (Act I, Scene 2, 114-117)

During the course of the play, the relationship between the images develops greater significance as those characters who take the equation too literally are all made to look ridiculous. Baptista's plans for Bianca's marriage are thwarted. Gremio, who has nothing but wealth to offer, is deceived. Hortensio is defied at the end of the play by his ''wealthy widow.'' In the case of Petruchio and Katharina, however, the equation becomes a measure of love's value when Katharina expresses her devotion to her husband in financial terms. In marriage, she says, the husband cares for his wife,

> And craves no other tribute at thy hands
> But love, fair looks, and true obedience —
> Too little payment for so great a debt.
> Such duty as the subject owes the prince,
> Even such a woman oweth to her husband.
>
> (Act V, Scene 2, 157-161)

Clothes and Character

Stage costume and clothing imagery are used by Shakespeare throughout his works as a measure either of the inward man or of the deceptions he practises on other people or on himself. In *The Taming of the Shrew,* much use is made of this relationship for a variety of purposes. Petruchio's assumed wildness is projected by means of clothes. He sees his preparations for his wedding in terms of clothing:

> . . . I will unto Venice
> To buy apparel 'gainst the wedding-day.
> . . .
> We will have rings, and things, and fine array.
>
> (Act II, Scene 1, 316-317, 325)

Normality is transgressed as he arrives for his wedding looking like "a monster, a very monster in apparel." His words underline the parallel between dress and character:

> To me she's married, not unto my clothes.
> Could I repair what she will wear in me
> As I can change these poor accoutrements,
> 'Twere well for Kate and better for myself.
>
> (Act III, Scene 2, 113-116)

This idea is further developed in the scenes at Petruchio's country house and becomes a source of physical comedy in the exchanges with the tailor and haberdasher. Again, Petruchio states the normal practice:

> . . . And now, my honey love,
> Will we return unto thy father's house,
> And revel it as bravely as the best,
> With silken coats and caps and golden rings,
> With ruffs and cuffs and farthingales and things;
> With scarfs and fans and double change of brav'ry.
>
> (Act IV, Scene 3, 52-57)

Then, after verbally reducing the clothes brought for his inspection to "a rag, a remnant . . . mere masquing stuff," he can point out the lesson:

> Our purses shall be proud, our garments poor:
> For 'tis the mind that makes the body rich;
> And as the sun breaks through the darkest clouds
> So honor peereth in the meanest habit.
>
> (Act IV, Scene 3, 168-171)

In the subplot, too, clothes imagery is used, chiefly as the measure of the deceptions practised. Tranio puts on his master's "colored hat and cloak" when he assumes his identity. It is his new clothes that Vincentio first notices on meeting him: "O fine villain! A silken doublet, a velvet hose, a scarlet cloak, and a copatain hat!" (Act V, Scene 1, 63-64). To ensure the success of the deception, Lucentio is disguised as the pedant, Cambio, Hortensio as the musician, Licio, and the pedant as Vincentio.

90

Household Management and Wifely Disorder

By theatrical and social tradition, dining and entertainment are symbolic of peace, concord and respect. While Katharina is shrewish, it is in terms of these functions that she is taught the implications of her behavior. First, she is dragged away from the feast celebrating her own wedding. Then, her reception in her new home turns out to be less than hospitable: there is no man at the door to take her horse and "no regard, no attendance, no duty." As the scene proceeds, the entertainment is turned by Petruchio into a slapstick display of violence in which pitchers are upset, dishes thrown about and food rejected as unfit and "choleric." We are also assured by Petruchio at the end of Act III, Scene 3 that Katharina's first night's rest shall be constantly disturbed in a mockery of care and attention. Later (Act IV, Scene 3), Grumio drives home the lesson as he torments her with the promise of food. Petruchio then offers her a small portion of meat that is quickly removed.

Shakespeare's Handling of the Shrew Theme

The central situation, the conflict between a shrewish wife and her husband, had for centuries been a popular literary theme in plays, ballads, jestbooks and tales. Shakespeare's treatment of it, however, was different from any previous one. He saw, in what had usually been treated as a primitive farcical action, the materials for a dramatic exploration of the relationship between the sexes in general and of the bases of marriage in particular.

Shakespeare widened the scope of his subject by characteristically blending with the shrew-taming theme quite dissimilar materials that he derived from other sources: the subplot concerning love and intrigue was taken from the sophisticated Italian-Classical tradition and the Induction that frames the whole was founded on the observation of contemporary English rustic life. One way to approach the meaning of the play is to examine the interrelationships among these three plot strands.

At the heart of the play's structure, there are two courtships and two marriages, which are quite obviously contrasted with each other. The one courtship is rough and farcical, the other, idealized and romantic. Katharina, the heroine of the first, is unnatural and shrewish and must be treated violently and cruelly in order to be brought to submission by a man who openly announces his intention "to wive it wealthily in Padua." In contrast, Bianca, her sister, is cast in a more conventional mould. Gentle and obedient, she is won by the idealistic devotion of a young man who is quite lacking in material motives.

This surface impression, however, is misleadingly simple because our initial attitudes toward the characters are reversed as the play proceeds. To begin with, Shakespeare endows his shrew with a dimension of humanity that is absent in her literary predecessors. He suggests, even during her outrageous behavior in the early scenes, that there are reasons for her state of mind. Her father's obvious favoritism, her jealousy of her younger sister's success and her frustration at not being married half persuade us that her violent reactions may be at least partially justified. In fact, it is easy to see in Katharina a girl whose pride has been outraged and who has allowed her "inflated proudmindedness" to take control of her whole being.

Petruchio is the one character in the play who understands

the reasons behind Katharina's actions. His behavior in courtship and marriage is calculated simply to force Katharina to realize herself what she has allowed to happen. His consciously assumed "wildness" both parallels and cures its unconsciously adopted counterpart in his wife.

Thus, out of violent and open conflict, these two characters forge a relationship that is not really based on the husband's tyranny and the wife's submission, but rather on self-knowledge and a final tolerance. By the end of the play, Katharina can gently poke fun at her husband's lunatic whims, seeing them for what they are: "But sun it is not, when you say it is not, / And the moon changes even as your mind." Yet, at the same time, she can also see her own former faults in a similar perspective:

> My mind hath been as big as one of yours,
> My heart as great, my reason haply more,
> To bandy word for word and frown for frown.
> (Act V, Scene 2, 175-177)

In offering to place her hand beneath her husband's foot, she knows that this is now the last sacrifice he requires of her; instead of accepting her offer, he wishes the seal of their newly won relationship: "Come on, and kiss me, Kate, . . . we'll to bed."

The Taming of the Shrew as Farce

The Taming of the Shrew is a farce, usually acted on the modern stage in playful, tongue-in-cheek fashion while the audience responds noisily to the antics of the performers.

The farce was originally used to fill in the interludes between the parts of a play and was an exaggerated comedy intended to be absurd and ridiculous, often satirical. Later, whole plays were woven around such a theme, to be taken lightly, not seriously. Three of Shakespeare's plays that are almost entirely farcical are *The Taming of the Shrew, The Merry Wives of Windsor* and *The Comedy of Errors*. Others that contain farcical elements in their comic subplots are *A Midsummer Night's Dream, Much Ado About Nothing, Measure for Measure, Twelfth Night, The Merchant of Venice* and *Henry IV* (Falstaff). There are even short comic interludes in the great tragedies, like the gravedigging scene in *Hamlet* and the porter scene in *Macbeth*.

In spite of the fact that the theme of *The Taming of the Shrew*, masculine supremacy and feminine submission, is distasteful to most modern readers, particularly women, the play itself is in such a rollicking mood that the audience is usually carried away with it, forgetting all objections in the delight of the farce. Before the end of the nineteenth century, it was the most often performed of Shakespeare's comedies and, of all his plays, second only to *Othello* in popularity. It still is one of the most frequently acted dramas.

The Taming of the Shrew presents a variety of stage tricks: mistaken identity, both with and without the aid of disguise; puns and twisted meanings galore; physical violence; love at first sight; a play within a play; music; animals; lessons to be learned; a practical joke or two; and three different but distinctive marriages.

Since farce depends on situation rather than on characterization, it offers little room for development of human beings, according to Marchette Chute. Presented in Elizabethan times against hangings and without scenery, the clever lines and sustained action kept the audience in suspense and filled with mirth and laughter. Such is still the case today.

Other Shakespearean Farces

A play is a comedy when the action ends favorably for the protagonist, or leading character. Most comedies are light and amusing, with a happy conclusion of the plot, a non-tragic ending. Polonius in *Hamlet* enumerates the various forms of drama: "tragedy, comedy, pastoral, pastoral-comical, tragical-historical, tragical-comical-historical-pastoral." Pastoral refers to having the scene out of doors. Only *Cymbeline* can qualify in all four of these categories. *Measure for Measure* and *All's Well That Ends Well* are "dark" comedies — that is, if they had had an ending less favorable, they would have been tragedies. Some brighter comedies are *The Merchant of Venice, As You Like It* and *Twelfth Night.* Still lighter in tone are the farces.

Farce is exaggerated comedy, intended to be absurd and ridiculous. It is based on broadly humorous situations and is not to be taken seriously. Often it includes slapstick and unheard of goings-on that could not occur in any other type of drama. Its purpose is to excite laughter, and great latitude is allowed as to the probability of happenings and naturalness of characters.

Three of Shakespeare's comedies are farces: *The Merry Wives of Windsor, The Taming of the Shrew* and *The Comedy of Errors.* Mark Van Doren suggests that there may be a fourth one, *Titus Andronicus,* which, for all its horror and cruelty, is as unfeeling as the mirth of the other three. Several other plays contain some farcical scenes of exaggerated humor intended to be absurd and ridiculous.

The Comedy of Errors is farce at its height. The plot, based on *Menaechmi* of Plautus, involves two sets of male twins, the Antipholus twins and their Dromio servants. Like *The Tempest, The Comedy of Errors* opens with a shipwreck, or rather a long-winded description of one, by Aegeon, father of the missing Antipholus twins. Shipwreck was a favorite device of Shakespeare, and one which he used also in *Twelfth Night, Pericles, Othello, The Merchant of Venice* and *The Winter's Tale.*

The most boisterous farce of all, and the only one written in prose, is *The Merry Wives of Windsor.* Disguise plays a conspicuous part here. Ford passes himself off as Brook to Falstaff in order to keep informed about the latter's procedure with his wife. Falstaff is once concealed in a buck basket, carried out of Ford's house and thrown into the Thames, thereby furnishing great sport for Mesdames Page and Ford and the merry wives. Again, in the dress of the old witch of Brentford, he receives an unmerciful beating at the hand of Ford. Last, but not least, is the final scene of the play, in which most of the characters appear masked.

Second only to *The Merry Wives* in the loudness of its slapstick comedy, of course, is *The Taming of the Shrew. A Midsummer Night's Dream* also contains farcical elements in its comic subplot, in which Peter Quince, Bottom, Starveling, Snout and the others rehearse their version of Pyramus and Thisbe and present it "on the Duke's wedding day at night." *Much Ado About Nothing* borders on farce with its spirited lovemaking of Beatrice and Benedick. *Measure for Measure,* dark and somber comedy that it is, has a slight but farcical subplot dealing with the misdemeanors of shady characters such as Pompey, Licio and Mistress Overdone. *Twelfth Night* has a subplot which practically overshadows the main plot, for much of the farce is built around the practical joke which the pranksters play on Malvolio. The Gobbos, father and son, furnish farcical amusement in *The Merchant of Venice* and, of course, Falstaff and his unsavory companions who surround Prince Hal add light-hearted humor to *Henry IV.* Even the deep tragedies have touches of farce. Witness Capulet's instructions to the servants and the robust character of the Nurse in *Romeo and Juliet.* Shakespeare knew just when to use farce as a foil for deep emotion as well as when to make it the tenor of the play itself.

*The Battle of the Sexes

When Petruchio the woman-hater is asked what gale blows him from Verona to Padua he answers airily, being a free and happy fellow with no other care than the need to find himself a wealthy wife:

> Such wind as scatters young men through the world
> To seek their fortunes farther than at home
> Where small experience grows.
>
> (Act I, Scene 2, 50-2)

The hilarious piece of which he is hero might so far, then, be such an excursion into the romantic universe of young Italian adventure as *The Two Gentlemen of Verona* is; for that experiment, of about the same age as *The Shrew,* starts also with youthful blades whetting their edges on the wheel of travel.

But Petruchio is hero of a farce, not of a romance. Comedy is made once more from situation: a shrew is to be tamed, a man is found to tame her, and he proceeds to do so by as many devices as can be developed in the time available. The interest of the audience will be in the devices, not in the persons who work them or upon whom they are worked. A certain callousness will be induced to form in the sensibilities of the beholder, so that whereas in another case he would be outraged he will now laugh freely and steadily for two hours. The practitioner in farce, no less than the practitioner in melodrama, must possess the art of insulating his audience's heart so that it cannot be shocked while the machinery hums.

The Taming of the Shrew, however, has a deep and curious interest such as *The Comedy of Errors* nowhere has. Formally it is as much a farce, and leans as frankly on a doctrine which Shakespeare must have adopted in cold blood, for on the evidence of the other plays it was not his own. This is the doctrine of male superiority, which Luciana had expressed in *The Comedy of Errors* when she reminded Adriana that men "are masters to their females" (Act II, Scene 1, 24), and which Petruchio expresses here not only when he declares of Katherine that

---

*Editor's title. From *Shakespeare,* by Mark Van Doren (New York: Henry Holt, 1939).

> She is my goods, my chattels; she is my house,
> My household stuff, my field, my barn,
> My horse, my ox, my ass, my any thing.
>
> (Act III, Scene 2, 232-4)

but indeed at all times and by all his actions; nor does Katherine fail at the end to agree. Yet the resulting play, as its popularity attests, is strangely and permanently interesting.

This is because it has hit the relation of the sexes at its liveliest point. Shakespeare hit the point again, and classically for him, in the story of Beatrice and Benedick; but even now he is master of the theme that lies in the war between love and pride, in the perhaps perversely fascinating spectacle of intellect and will being brought into line with instinct. Love stories are never so engaging as when their principals do not wish to love, and particularly when it is their power that prevents them. For one thing, we are never so sure as then that love is genuine; and for another, there is a peculiar delight in discovering that two persons have mistaken attraction for repulsion, and in listening to the reverse language of raillery which they employ in place of lisps and sighs. The best lovers are witty lovers who bury their perturbation under abuse; at least this is true for comedy, and by all means it is the case where situation is the thing.

Our secret occupation as we watch *The Taming of the Shrew* consists of noting the stages by which both Petruchio and Katherine — both of them, for in spite of everything the business is mutual — surrender to the fact of their affection. Shakespeare has done this not by violating his form, not by forgetting at any point to write farce, and least of all by characterizing his couple. He has left them man and woman, figures for whom we can substitute ourselves, and that is precisely what we do as we commence to understand why Katherine wants so badly to hear Bianca talk of her suitors, even beats her because she will not; as we read reservations into her scorn of Petruchio; as we wait to see her give Petruchio (Act V, Scene 1) his first quiet kiss; and as we assume behind Petruchio's roughness a growing attachment to this woman he is so deliciously — we must confess it — torturing. Shakespeare has done what he has done somewhat as a general takes a city: by sheer strength, in utter confidence, and with the soundest knowledge of our outstanding weakness.

Both the man and the woman are brilliant of tongue. She

can call him "a mad-cap ruffian and a swearing Jack," "a frantic fool," "a mad-brain rudesby." But his high spirits carry him as far as genius. His anger, real or pretended, leads him to the limits of language:

> You peasant swain! You whoreson malt-horse drudge!
> (Act IV, Scene 1, 132)

> A whoreson beetle-headed, flap-ear'd knave!
> (Act IV, Scene 1, 160)

> Why, this was moulded on a porringer. . . .
> Why, 't is a cockle or a walnut-shell,
> A knack, a toy, a trick, a baby's cap.
> (Act IV, Scene 3, 64-7)

> Why, thou say'st true; it is a paltry cap,
> A custard-coffin, a bauble, a silken pie.
> (Act IV, Scene 3, 81-2)

> What's this? A sleeve? 'T is like a demi-cannon.
> What, up and down, carv'd like an apple-tart?
> Here's snip and nip and cut and slish and slash,
> Like to a censer in a barber's shop.
> (Act IV, Scene 3, 88-91)

The language of the play, or at any rate of the play as it concerns Katherine and Petruchio, is everywhere vigorous and vernacular, and healthily grown over with tough local terms. We hear of a chestnut in a farmer's fire, of boys with bugs, of hazel-twigs and hazel nuts, of kersey boot-hose, of horses shoulder-shotten and begnawn with the bots, of sops thrown in the sexton's face, of apples and oysters, of a bottom of brown thread, of rush-candles, and of parsley in the garden to stuff a rabbit. Petruchio's crowning harangue against the tailor is stuck as full of such terms as a ham with cloves:

> Thou liest, thou thread, thou thimble,
> Thou yard, three-quarters, half-yard, quarter, nail!
> Thou flea, thou nit, thou winter-cricket thou! . . .
> Away, thou rag, thou quantity, thou remnant.
> (Act IV, Scene 3, 107-12)

But the servants also are accomplished in the speech of their region, which it goes without saying is not Italy. And the Induction, wherein Christophero Sly awakes from his sleep to be Bottom in a lord's bedchamber, is as local as an inn-yard , a broken fence, a yawning dog, with its talk of old Sly's son of Burton Heath, Marian Hacket the fat ale-wife of Wincot, Peter Turph, and Henry Pimpernell. The Induction contains several of Shakespeare's later themes — music, the voices of hounds, dreams and delusions, and instructions to players; but significantly enough they are restrained within the bounds of farce, they are enriched with none of the later meaning. The hounds are hunting-dogs, music is a household affair, and dreams are funny.

But the comedy has never strayed from its path, unless the insipid second story of Bianca and her suitors is to be considered an attempt, by Shakespeare or by someone else, to save the whole for romance. It is not saved. A play in which the heroine can be called a devil, a wench, a fiend of hell, a rotten apple, a thing to be boarded, an irksome brawling scold, a wildcat, and in which we nevertheless take the purest pleasure, has in fact been saved but saved as farce. How otherwise could we behold so callously the wringing of ears and the knocking of heads which appear to be Petruchio's natural habits — and his servants', and Katherine's, for she ties her sister's hands and strikes at least three persons before she settles down? As for the settling down, there is that last long speech of hers in which she declares the humble duty of a wife in terms which would be painful to us were she a person as Portia and Imogen are persons. Katherine is a shrew. She has been tamed. And the logic of farce is that she should say so.

Selected Criticisms

. . . Katharina's speech on the duty of wives and the paying of 'tribute' is joyful and elated because, in some mysterious way, she has confidence in Petruchio's love and in his willingness to give away his loan of Nature's bounty. There is no doubt at the end of *The Shrew* that he or she who gives most, not in the terms of commercial wealth but in terms of the contract of love, must inevitably get most. To present the happiness of this contract in lively dramatic terms is the great achievement of *The Shrew*. It is sometimes called a brutal and degrading play, but this could only be true if Katharina's submission had been abject, or if Petruchio, in triumph, had put his foot upon her hand; what happens, in fact, is that Petruchio and Katharina exchange kisses and her speech is confident and joyful, the most sustained and spirited speech in the whole play. Viewed against Shakespeare's ideal of love's wealth, this comedy presents, in its own gay, hilarious way, a profound mystery — how in love 'Property was thus appalled,' how 'Either was the other's mine.'

John Russell Brown, Shakespeare and His Comedies, 1957.

It seems needless to dwell at any length upon the characterization in *The Shrew*. The figures in the subplot are the conventional characters of classic comedy: The lover, the artful servant, a pair of old fathers, and the girl who is the cause of all the trouble. In the main plot Grumio plays a clown's role akin to that of Sander in *A Shrew*, but we may note that Shakespeare carefully cut down this part: his Grumio is the subordinate comic servant, not the semi-independent Clown of older comedy.

The transformation that Shakespeare worked upon the hero and heroine of the main plot has already been noted, and it is just this transformation combined with lively action that has given *The Shrew* its extraordinary vitality on the stage. Petruchio and Katherine are capital acting parts, but they are something more. They are representative figures in the eternal duel of the sexes, each endowed with personality and strength enough to carry a vigorous contest to a happy conclusion.

It is in this combat, this clash of wills, that the true dramatic value of *The Shrew* consists. In the hands of a modern dramatist it might easily have reached a tragic conclusion. But Shakespeare was no Ibsen; it was probably a psychical impossibility for him to conceive a Kate turning her back on her husband and slamming the door after her as she goes out into the world. For him to have entertained such a conception would have been to break with a medieval convention of long standing. We have already seen how Noah and his sons use physical force to get his recalcitrant wife into the Ark; and Tom Tyler calls in a friend to beat his shrewish wife into temporary submission. In a rude ballad, "A Merry Jest of a Shrewd and Curst Wife," extant in Shakespeare's youth, the shrew is not only well beaten, but finally wrapped in the salted hide of an old horse. It is to the credit of the author of *A Shrew* that he disdains this sort of "merry jest"; Ferando never lays a hand on Kate; no more does Petruchio, though once he threatens jestingly to return the blow she gives him with a counterbuff. Shakespeare, who knew all about hawks, knew better than to make Petruchio try to tame his haggard by the use of force; his explosions of violence are wordy rather than physical, directed at others rather than at Kate, and they are, in effect, comic exaggerations of her own fierce insistence upon her will. Kate is keen-sighted enough to see the absurdity of her husband's behavior and, when at last she comes to recognize it as a fantastic distortion of her own, she is ready to renounce the role of a virago and assume that of an obedient and loving wife. To lament, as some modern critics do, the ruin of a strong character under the impact of brute force is to turn Shakespeare's merry play into a psychological tragedy. The psychology of *The Shrew*, such as it is, is Elizabethan, not Freudian. Kate's shrewishness is an Elizabethan 'humor' and, as one of the servants, like a kind of Chorus, aptly remarks, Petruchio "kills her in her own humor." *The Taming of the Shrew* is an Elizabethan comedy, but it retains its comic value even today. It still is not well for the wife to wear the breeches, and the triumphant tour of Lunt and Fontanne in this play reveals an American audience readier to understand Shakespeare than some of his critics.

Thomas Marc Parrott, Shakespearean Comedy, 1962.

We begin, then, with the Induction, which clearly aims at providing the main comic plot with a setting which at once limits it, isolating it from normal reality, and serves in some measure to comment upon it. Compared with Sly's mixture of boorishness and ignorance, all the characters of the main action in Padua are creatures of the stage, instruments of theatrical illusion; and this, perhaps, is worth remembering if, at a later stage, we are tempted to take too seriously Petruchio's brutal treatment of Katherine or to deduce from it too directly a primitive and inhuman attitude towards women. Sly stands to the main comic theme in the same relationship as we, being spectators, stand to the actors performing before us on the stage; he is placed on a different plane, a different level of reality, precisely to stress the element of artifice and make-believe in the rest. The device, though carried out with a good deal less than complete consistency, represents a considerable advance in Shakespeare's conception of the effects which his comedy could compass.

Sly himself, moreover, is a figure of some potential subtlety. In the course of his brief appearance he is imaginatively translated, carried in his own despite to a new world of the imagination. His resistance to this process, and the weakening of it, are interestingly portrayed. We may notice in this connection how the luxury to which he awakes from his drunken sleep, and which is expressed by those who surround him in a high-flown parody of the resounding Marlovian line:

> wilt thou sleep? we'll have thee to a couch
> Softer and sweeter than the lustful bed
> On purpose trimm'd up for Semiramis.
> Say thou wilt walk: we will bestrew the ground;
> Or wilt thou ride? thy horses shall be trapp'd,
> Their harness studded all with gold and pearl.
> Dost thou love hawking? thou hast hawks will soar
> Above the morning lark —
>
> (Induction 2)

is contrasted with the prose plainness of: "What, would you make me mad? Am not I Christopher Sly, old Sly's son of Burton-heath, by birth a pedlar, by education a card-maker, by transmutation a bear-herd, and now by present profession a tinker?" If we read the verse passage in isolation we shall probably conclude that Marlowe often did these things better; but the setting of the Lord's rhetoric against the tinker's plain prose, and the establishment of this contrast as an essential part of the comic effect, is Shakespeare's own. Nor is Sly allowed to stand upon this initial position. The development which takes place in him from unbelief to absorbtion in a dream which reality appears to confirm:

I do not sleep: I see, I hear, I speak;
I smell sweet savours and I feel soft things:
Upon my life, I am a lord indeed,
And not a tinker nor Cristofero Sly —

(Induction 2)

is managed with some subtlety and contributes to the balance of
reality and illusion, gross absurdity and a certain precarious
imaginative transformation, at which the whole episode aims.
Finally, Sly's closing references to the page whom he believes to
be his new 'wife' and to the 'obedience' which she owes him,
stand in a more direct relationship to the main themes of the
following comedy.

Derek Traversi, *Shakespeare: The Early Comedies*, 1964.

Accustomed as we now are to find more and more subtleties
in Shakespeare, most of us are emotionally inclined to credit
Petruchio with considerable delicacy and perceptiveness of feeling under his violent exterior and we shall meet abundant cor-
roboration for being so inclined. It is also to the interest of the
play that Petruchio should thus illustrate decisively the master
theme of appearance and reality. Let me illustrate Petruchio's
delicacy or perceptiveness. In the long courting scene (Act II,
Scene 1), when Petruchio and Katherina have their contest of
wits, Petruchio shows delicacy of feeling in giving her the chance
of saving her face before the rest if she should change her tune
and accept him quietly, for he says to Baptista, "If she be curst,
it is for policy," and follows this up with "'Tis bargained 'twixt
us twain, being alone,/That she shall be curst in company." In
the same context Petruchio keeps on referring to Katherina's
beauty; and it may be legitimate to suppose that in so doing he
adopts a policy towards her that her family had been foolish to
omit. Then there are his reiterated suggestions of sharing; that
they are really at one if only she would see it. His outrageous
clothes at the wedding are an emblem that proclaims: these are to
my true self what your own shrewishness is to your true self; and
each as well as the other can change the assumed self for the true
one. This is what Petruchio means when he says, just before the
wedding, "To me she's married, not unto my clothes"; and at
once Tranio ratifies the emblematic quality of those clothes with,
"He hath some meaning in his mad attire." And when after the

wedding the taming begins in earnest, the sharing continues. If Katherina has a cold rough journey to the country house, so has Petruchio. If she is deprived of supper, so is he also. And he speaks of them jointly suffering choler:

> And better 'twere that both of us did fast,
> Since, of ourselves, ourselves are choleric,
> Than feed it with such over-roasted flesh . . .
> And for this night we'll fast for company.
>
> (Act IV, Scene 1)

And he shows much patience in bearing with her stupidity when she will not see the game he has been playing. If she could not recognize the game when Petruchio abuses the haberdasher over the cap, at least when he repeats the game with the tailor, she should have seen it and consented to join in. And when she insists on putting him right on the time of day, his patience in not abandoning the game is almost saintly.

E. M. W. Tillyard, Shakespeare's Early Comedies, 1965.

The Taming of the Shrew has often been read and acted as a wife-humiliating farce in which a brute fortune-hunter carries all, including his wife's spirit, before him. But it is not so at all. True, it is based on the medieval conception of the obedience owed by a wife to her wedded lord, a conception generously and charmingly asserted by Katerina at the end. But it is a total misconception to suppose she has been bludgeoned into defeat. Indeed if either of them has triumphed in the art and practice of happy marriage, it is she.

Why is she a shrew? Shakespeare prepares us perfectly for this aspect of her character. She is a girl of spirit, forced to endure a father who is ready to sell his daughters to the highest bidder (as we see in the marriage-market scene, Act II, Scene 1) and who has made a favourite of her sly little sister. What choice has Katerina but to show her disdainful temper if she is to keep her self-respect?

Petruchio is a self-admitted fortune-hunter, but he is also good-natured, vigorous, candid, humorous, and likeable. No doubt whatever is left that he admires Katerina for herself on sight. Though he is loud-mouthed and swaggering, he is not contemptible; to Katerina he must have seemed her one hope of escape from that horrible family, against which she had developed the defensive technique of shrewishness; it is this which Petruchio is determined to break in her, not her spirit; and he chooses the method of practical joking to do so.

Neville Coghill, "The Basis of Shakespearean Comedy,"
Shakespeare Criticism 1935-1960, 1970.

In *The Taming of the Shrew* as in *The Comedy of Errors*, Shakespeare utilizes an external framing device to establish the spectator's comic distance. Even though in its present form the action of the Induction is never concluded, quite probably Sly and his attendants are intended to remain on the balcony stage throughout the play to observe the action below. Thus the scene serves constantly to draw the filter of fiction before us lest we be tempted to forget that Kate is a purely artificial figure of farce and, like many an armchair critic, to become indignant that Shakespeare could consider such cruel mistreatment of womankind as comic. The lord, returning from his hunting expedition and spying the drunken Sly sprawled in front of an alehouse, determines to "practice on this drunken man" by surrounding him with lavish ornaments and convincing him he is a rich man who has for years suffered from loss of memory and obsession with poverty. The playwright, as if to provide double comic insurance, depicts now the arrival of players who, after consulting with the lord, agree to perform a shrew story, "pleasing stuff," for Sly's entertainment. Finally, the lord proclaims that he will act to control the reasonable limits of the humor:

> haply my presence
> May well abate the over-merry spleen
> Which otherwise would grow into extremes.
>
> (Induction 1, 136-138)

Shortly after the major action is underway, the characters of the Induction again appear to remind us of a play watched by Sly, who in turn is presumably watched by a lord, and who in turn is observed by us. Groggy and nodding, Sly awakens barely long enough to mumble to his page-wife: " 'Tis a very excellent piece of work madam lady; would 'twere done!" (Act I, Scene 1, 258-259)

106

The major device for creating comic distance, then, like the protatic action involving Aegeon and Aemilia in *The Comedy of Errors*, is a layer of material entirely outside the main action. The machinery may indeed be crude when compared with the techniques which Shakespeare is to develop in his subsequent work, but the result is firmly to establish the perspective for situation comedy.

Larry S. Champion, *The Evolution of Shakespeare's Comedy*, 1970.

The Taming of A Shrew is predominantly satirical in spirit; for not only is its main plot a caricature of an eccentric woman and her no less eccentric tamer, but the subplot also with its extravagant romantic verbiage sounds as a mockery of romantic courtship appropriately placed beside the main business of shrew-taming. And the tinker's resolve to practise the lesson in shrew-taming in his own house brings the satiric import even more sharply into focus. Gascoigne's *Supposes*, from which Shakespeare derived materials for his subplot, is a comedy of extravagant intrigues in which the hero, who has an irregular union with his lady-love in the disguise of a servant, is imprisoned in a dark cell, while his servant impersonates him as a rival in wooing of an old man, who is at last discovered to be the servant's father. Besides these absurdly improbable situations, there is also a touch of romance in the unswerving loyalty of the lover and the sentimentalism of the mistress.

Though Shakespeare has adopted the central story of shrew-taming from the source play more or less closely, he has introduced an emotional element which takes away from the crudity of the rough taming and makes it partly a romantic drama of love, which is not always smooth in its course. The subplot, too, in spite of the puzzling situations which are reminiscent of classical comedy, is pre-eminently romantic, though it must be admitted that in this early play the two stories — of Katharina and Bianca — stand apart and have not been fused into a unity. Satire and fantasy seldom go well together.

The play's lack of internal harmony is reflected also in the dramatic content. The different strands of the play have not been illuminated by a central significance: the Induction, for instance, is unrelated to the main theme, and the cumbrous intrigue in the subplot, that of passing the Pedant off as Lucentio's father, is not quite compatible with the story of romantic courtship. It may only be said that *The Taming of The Shrew* is a comedy of marriage which embraces a rich variety of wooing, ranging from the barbaric and the mercenary to the romantic. But what emerges in the final impression is that the mode of wooing has little bearing on the winning of the heart, which has its own mysterious ways.

Dinesh Biswas, *Shakespeare's Treatment of His Sources*, 1971.

. . . Petruchio and Katharina are not the ludicrous stereotypes we expect in farce. Katharina in particular is a magnificent creation — a prototype for such later misanthropic heroines as Beatrice and Isabella. She illustrates all the evil potentialities of soured virtue summed up in the concluding line of Sonnet 94: "Lilies that fester smell far worse than weeds." Unlike Bianca, who affects a coy mask to conceal her egotism, Katharina's more legitimate sense of her own merits has turned her resentment at their neglect into shrewishness. There is something of the tragic obtuseness of a Hotspur or a Coriolanus in her fiery independence of convention:

Why, sir, I trust I may have leave to speak;
And speak I will; I am no child, no babe:
Your betters have endured me say my mind,
And if you cannot, best you stop your ears.
My tongue will tell the anger of my heart,
Or else my heart concealing it will break,
And rather than it shall, I will be free
Even to the uttermost, as I please, in words.

(Act IV, Scene 3, 73-80)

A modern mind instinctively sympathizes with such sincerity, and so does Shakespeare, self-destructive though he knows it to be. This dangerous forthrightness and promptness distinguish his most dynamic figures — Othello, Cordelia, Kent, even Lear — but it is precisely their lack of "Machiavellian" flexibility which dooms such characters. Katharina's virtue is that she has retained a capacity for suppleness, even though she clearly begins the play in a neurotic state of mind. Her beating of the bound Bianca (Act II, Scene 1, 21) is obviously pathological; and even her wit has a strain of physical violence (Act II, Scene 1, 22off.) which implies a mind close to breakdown. Thus, like Christopher Sly, her disintegrating personality seems to justify almost any kind of shock therapy; and it is the virtue of Petruchio to grasp that a personality of her aggressiveness necessarily possesses enormous possibilities. Petruchio brings to his unconventional choice of a wife all the mature skepticism and contempt for sentimental expectations in love which appear in the most subtle of Shakespeare's sonnets praising the unconventional attractions of the Dark Lady.

Hugh Richmond, Shakespeare's Sexual Comedy, 1971.

. . . A character of stature is the kind of character in whom we could easily take a serious interest, the kind of character with whose consciousness our own consciousness could easily become continuous. But once a comic dramatist decides upon the use of a character of stature he must do two things. First, he must establish such a character within the frame of a comic point of view. Secondly, he must carefully control the development of the character so that it does not exceed limits which are appropriate to the world which the character inhabits. In the case of a farce such as *The Taming of the Shrew* this means that Petruchio's development must be very carefully controlled, since in terms of stature he is about as much as a farce can take. A farce, by definition, depends a great deal on physicality and is not concerned to involve us in substantial psychological complexity. And yet if a farce is merely physical or is confined to the use of static characters it is bound to be dull. Mere physicality is not enough if a comic point of view and a view of reality are to be shaped into a meaningful whole. A lasting farce carefully balances its necessary physicality with some representation of persistent social species whose destiny is both to go on revealing themselves to us and to suggest meanings substantially beyond their identity as social species or type characters.

Our view of Petruchio's character appropriately divides into five parts. The first is the opening definition of character as he arrives in Padua (Act I, Scene 2, Act II, Scene 1). The second is his verbal duel with Kate and its aftermath (Act II, Scene 1). The third is a brief transition (Act III). The fourth is the group of taming scenes with Kate in his country house and the subsequent encounter with Vincentio in which the taming process is brought to its successful conclusion (Act IV, Scenes 1, 3, 5). The fifth is the concluding scene of the play.

William J. Martz, Shakespeare's Universe of Comedy, 1971.

Sport, playacting, education — the taming of Katharina is not finally any of these things, but something *sui generis*, the working out of a personal relationship. But these other activities are analogous, and are placed in the play as points of reference. The achievement of "peace . . . , and love, and quiet life" (Act V, Scene 1, 108) in Petruchio's marriage is seen as part of a whole range of activities whereby men try to bring order and pleasure into their lives. In showing this, the play also shows us as creatures of convention: our most pleasurable activities are organized, limited, bounded by rules; and Petruchio's ultimate lesson may be that order and pleasure are inseparable. We also load ourselves with superficial conventions: the play identifies romantic love and a stuffy sense of propriety as two of these, and comically explodes them. But sport and playacting — both highly conventionalized activities — are seen as genuine sources of strength and enjoyment, and Petruchio's application of these activities to his marriage, while it may seem bizarre to the citizens of Padua, is triumphantly justified.

The characters of *The Comedy of Errors* and *The Two Gentlemen of Verona* are comically trapped by limited orders of understanding; they find it difficult, if not impossible, to rise out of their private worlds and see them in relation to other worlds (though Julia is to some degree an exception). But in *The Taming of the Shrew* Petruchio, Katherina and the Lord have a special vision, an awareness of life as a play or a game, that gives them a power to control not only their own lives but other people's. They have a sense of convention, and therefore a power to manipulate convention, to create experiences rather than have experiences forced upon them. The Lord in creating a new identity for Sly, Petruchio in creating a new life for Katherina, and she herself when she finally joins in this act of creation — all of them convey some of what we imagine to be their own creator's zest in the act of making a new world come to life.

Alexander Leggatt, Shakespeare's Comedy of Love, 1974.

Review Questions and Answers

Question 1.
For what purpose does Shakespeare include the Induction scenes?

Answer

By the use of the Induction scenes, Shakespeare removes *The Taming of the Shrew* one step away from the audience. Christopher Sly, the drunken Warwickshire tinker, is, like us, the audience of the play, and so constitutes a different level of reality from the actors of the play itself. His imagination is worked upon, so that he accepts as reality the illusion the lord forces upon him, even as Katharina accepts Petruchio's performance in order to learn reality. Our last view of him is as he sits, like Kate, "new-wakened from a dream," receiving as his wife a page who is dressed as a girl and who is all obedience.

Question 2.
How does the play portray Elizabethan marriage and court-ship customs?

Answer

Both of the marriages in the play are seen against the background of mating customs that are similar to those that prevailed in the England of Shakespeare's day. In their extreme form, they are represented by the money-minded Baptista, for whom marriage is primarily an economic arrangement, and by the old Gremio, who, by virtue of his great wealth, seeks to transgress the bounds of nature and marry a young wife. Both of these men, and presumably the standards they represent, are certainly defeated by the intriguing younger folk. Yet, as we have seen, it is not Bianca and Lucentio who, circumventing these mores, achieve a true relationship. Rather it is Petruchio and his shrew who, accepting them, work out a harmonious living arrangement within their limitations.

What Shakespeare has done, in effect, in this early play is to turn the traditional farce of shrew-taming into a comedy of human relationships. In his later comedies he was to return again and again to the same theme of what constitutes harmony between the sexes. And it is no accident that the most sparkling of

111

his comic lovers, Beatrice and Benedick of *Much Ado About Nothing,* should derive a great deal of their charm from the fact that their courtship, like Katharina and Petruchio's, is carried on by means of a conflict of wills.

Question 3.

How is the play a reflection of life in Shakespeare's England despite the supposedly Italian setting?

Answer

One may obtain a glimpse of life in Tudor England simply by paying attention to the background of *The Taming of the Shrew.* The vast gap between upper and lower classes is brought out in the Induction, as well as in Petruchio's lordly conduct before his servants and in Lucentio's friendly relations with his, although class barriers are never overstepped.

The English names used in the play — Christopher, John, Curtis, Adam, Cicely, Joan and Alice, for instance — are all familiar to the modern English-speaking world. Actual names of people and places in Warwickshire are used: Stephen Sly, Marian Hacket, Burton-on-Heath, Wincot and High Cross were all realities of Shakespeare's contemporary Stratford neighborhood.

Articles used and customs mentioned are English not Italian. References to foods and household goods create a picture of daily life. Among the many contemporary items mentioned are fustian (a coarse cloth), chestnuts, hazel nuts, kersey boot hose, rush-candles, a bottom of brown thread, beef and mustard, tripe, a neat's foot, rabbit and apple tart.

Even the speech of the characters, particularly the servants, reflects that of sixteenth-century Stratford. Fashions satirized in Act IV, Scene 3 are those worn by English ladies of the time. The Pegasus, an inn mentioned in Act IV, Scene 4, actually existed in London. The Italian setting, as in a dozen other Shakespearean plays, is purely nominal. The fabric of the play is clearly English.

Question 4.

Describe the contrast between the Katharina-Petruchio relationship and that of Bianca and Lucentio.

Answer

Against a vigorous, realistic conflict between the sexes (Katharina-Petruchio), Shakespeare sets the Bianca-Lucentio courtship and marriage. The attitudes and idiom that Lucentio adopts, in contrast with Petruchio's, are in keeping with those of the conventional romantic lover. He falls in love at first sight, and self-indulgently drops into wild verbal excess. He "burns," "pines," and "perishes" for love. Bianca becomes his goddess, with her "sweet beauty," "coral lips," and her breath that perfumes the air. All he sees in her is "sacred and sweet." Bianca herself is characterized in terms of the same convention. She is silent, modest, obedient, and desired — "the patroness of heavenly harmony," who takes delight only in music and poetry.

Yet, as the Bianca-Lucentio love affair develops, it becomes a thing of self-interest, intrigue, and deception. Lucentio's disguise as Cambio the schoolmaster is visually symbolic of this. Bianca's "obedient modesty" and apparent acquiescence to her father's wishes are seen to be merely a cover for her plans as she calmly sets about making her own marital arrangements. It is, consequently, no accident that Katharina's relationship with Petruchio in the final scene is sharply contrasted with Bianca and Lucentio's. As Katharina drags her rebellious sister into the banquet room, it is Lucentio who reproaches his new wife ruefully — "The wisdom of your duty, fair Bianca, / Hath cost one hundred crowns since supper time" — only to be told by his now changed goddess, "The more fool you, for laying on my duty."

Thus, by the end of the play, the two sisters have spiritually changed places, so that it is the former shrew who asserts the "true bias of nature," and the earlier patroness of music who provides the "harsh hearing" when women are "froward."

Question 5.
Compare Baptista to some of the other deceived father figures in Shakespeare's plays.

Answer
Baptista, like other fathers of Shakespeare's heroines — Egeus in *A Midsummer Night's Dream,* Capulet in *Romeo and Juliet* and even Prospero in *The Tempest* — is watchful of his daughters and eager to secure for them the best education and husbands available. He is short-sighted and easily duped, however, for he never suspects the elaborate deception going on around him, which culminates in the elopement of Bian-

ca with the real Lucentio. Tranio, the servant boy in his master's garb, is accepted at face value by Baptista and so is the masquerading pedant. Cambio and Licio enter, unquestioned, Baptista's house and employ. Mothers are usually absent from the Shakespeare plays, a stage device to give the young people, particularly the heroines, more freedom to act. Those few mothers included are often unfavorable characters, such as Lady Capulet and Queen Gertrude. Yet most of the comedies and many of the tragedies include a father, not always a powerful influence in the play. This is true of Baptista as well as of Leonato, Hero's father in *Much Ado About Nothing* and Brabantio, father of Desdemona in *Othello*. All these fathers, like the ruling officials (dukes, princes, etc.), are needed as background for the plot.

Question 6.

What does Tranio contribute to the play?

Answer

Tranio, amazingly resourceful, quick-thinking, and possessed of some veneer of culture, is the servant boy, who in difficult situations impersonates his master without faltering. He belongs with other sharp-witted servants in Shakespeare, including Maria in *Twelfth Night,* who could write so well that on a forgotten matter her handwriting could not be distinguished from that of her mistress, Olivia, and Nerissa in *The Merchant of Venice,* who is clever and refined enough to be more of a companion than a servant to Portia. Tranio must also possess a good physique and pleasing facial features. His deception of Baptista is complete, although Gremio is suspicious of the extravagant claims to money and property made by the supposed Lucentio. Tranio contributes much humor and entertainment to the play.

Question 7.

Trace the steps by which Shakespeare conveys Katharina's transition.

Answer

Katharina, of all Shakespeare's characters, shows the greatest improvement in behavior. This change is the result of outside pressure applied by another person, but it is, nevertheless, lasting. Willful, spoiled, overbearing and sharp-tongued, this handsome and wealthy young shrew yet secretly longs for a husband. She feels inferior and frustrated because of Bianca's numerous suitors and her own lack of acceptance as a candidate for the only career open to women, marriage. In a vicious circle, her bad temper becomes more pronounced as time goes by and no suitor bids for her.)

One does appear eventually. Through the conniving of Hortensio and Gremio, young Petruchio, amiable enough beneath the surface but stormy in outward demeanor, readily agrees to woo Katharina. By meeting fire with fire, he succeeds in reducing the fiery temper of Katharina to ashes from which emerges a new, loyal, obedient Kate, ready to become a model for other wives inclined to be "froward," for the shrew has fallen in love. The whole transformation of Kate is in a light vein, full of farce and fun. Without her, the play would be flat indeed, for her liveliness gives action and spark to this drama, which is one of Shakespeare's most often acted and absorbing plays.

Question 8.

Identify and provide examples of some figures of speech used in *The Taming of the Shrew*.

Answer

A *simile* is a comparison between two things and is usually introduced by "like" or "as."
Example:
. . . as he that leaves
A shallow plash to plunge him in the deep.

(Act I, Scene 1, 22-23)

A *metaphor* is a substitution of one thing for another, without the use of "like" or "as."
Example:
Our cake's dough on both sides.

(Act I, Scene 1, 109)

An *epigram* is a brief and pointed saying.
Example:
There's small choice in rotten apples.

(Act I, Scene 1, 138)

Hyperbole is an extreme exaggeration of the truth.
Example:
Why, so this gallant will command the sun.

(Act IV, Scene 3, 198)

Personification bestows on lifeless objects or ideas the qualities of persons.
Example:
I read that I profess, the Art of Love.

(Act IV, Scene 2, 7)

Apostrophe is direct address to a person or thing.
Example:
... thou thread, thou thimble ...

(Act IV, Scene 3, 108)

Irony contains a hidden meaning opposite to that expressed in words.
Example:
Say that she rail; why then I'll tell her plain
She sings as sweetly as a nightingale.

(Act II, Scene 1, 171-172)

Stichomythia is a rapid dialogue in single alternate lines, as in ancient Greek drama.
Example:
Pet: Come, come, you wasp; i' faith you are too angry.
Kath: If I be waspish, best beware my sting.

(Act II, Scene 1, 210-211)

A *pun,* or a play on words, is the humorous use of words that sound alike but are different in meaning.
Example:
Pet: Here sirrah Grumio; *knock,* I say.
Gru: Knock, sir! whom should I *knock*?

(Act I, Scene 2, 5-6)

Question 9.
Comment on the poetry and use of language in the play.

Answer

   The Taming of the Shrew is an early Shakespearean comedy which exhibits little of the rich poetic language found in his later, more sophisticated works. There are few purely lyrical passages in the play. For the most part, the language is straightforward and earthy, conveying meaning directly rather than through elaborate means of expression. The play does contain many images and figures of speech, but these are usually more functional and uncomplicated than the flights of lyricism characteristic of Shakespeare's more mature plays. Several of Lucentio's speeches can be considered purely poetic, but Shakespeare is here parodying the extravagant sentimentality of romantic love. The dialogue of the central characters in the play, Katharina and Petruchio, is perhaps less poetic than that of the subplot characters. However, the frank and sometimes coarse language of Katharina and Petruchio proves to be full of life, wit and interest, in contrast to the pale exchanges that take place between Lucentio and Bianca. It has been suggested that the vigorous blank verse of the central plot overshadows the stale poetry of the secondary plot because the playwright invested his energy in the portrayal of the unconventional characters, rather than the dull, commonplace characters. Those who believe that Shakespeare was not the sole author of *The Shrew* attribute the inferior quality of the language in the subplot material to another writer.

   In the Induction, the plain prose of Christopher Sly is in marked contrast to the formal blank verse spoken by the lord. Sly's use of dialect and homespun expressions reveals his lower class origins, while the lord's polished speech and use of hunting terms distinguishes him as one of noble birth.

Question 10.

   What purposes do the various disguises in the play serve?

Answer

   In the subplot of *The Taming of the Shrew,* many disguises are assumed. Hortensio poses as a tutor to woo Bianca secretly. Lucentio disguises himself as Cambio. Tranio assumes the identity of Lucentio. The pedant is persuaded to pretend that he is Vincentio.

   Other, non-literal forms of disguise are also assumed in the play. The characters in the main plot wear personality masks that conceal their real selves. Katharina poses as a shrew to disguise the hurt and frustration she suffers as a slighted daughter and a frequently rejected marriage prospect. She does not abandon her shrewish pretence until Petruchio brings her to a roundabout acceptance of her true self. In order to "tame" Katharina, however, Petruchio must also wear a mask. Although he pretends that his interest in Katharina is based purely on hopes of financial gain, the lengths he goes to in attempting to tame his bride prove that he is sincerely concerned about Katharina herself. By appreciating Katharina, Petruchio allows her to understand her self-worth and drop the mask of shrewishness. Petruchio also teaches her that clothes and external appearance are insignificant; what matters is the personality beneath these outward trappings.

Bianca and the widow also wear masks that conceal their true natures. Unlike Katharina, though, these two more conventional types of women disguise their shrewishness under a docile and submissive exterior. Their true natures are revealed in the concluding scene of the play when they exchange roles with Katharina.

Bibliography

Ashton, Florence H. "The Revision of the Folio Text of *The Taming of the Shrew*," Philological Quarterly, VI (1927).

Biswas, Dinesh. *Shakespeare's Treatment of His Sources.* Calcutta: Jadavpur University, 1971.

Brown, John Russell. *Shakespeare and His Comedies.* London: Methuen, 1957.

Champion, Larry S. *The Evolution of Shakespeare's Comedy.* Cambridge, Mass.: Harvard University Press, 1970.

Coghill, Nevill. "The Basis of Shakespearean Comedy," *Shakespeare Criticism 1935-1960*, ed. Ann Ridler. London: Oxford University Press, 1970.

Duthie, George I. *"The Taming of the Shrew and The Taming of a Shrew," Review of English Studies,* XIX (1943).

Draper, John. "Kate the Curst," *Journal of Mental and Nervous Diseases,* LXXXIX (1939).

Gray, Henry D. *"The Taming of the Shrew," Philological Quarterly*, XX (1941).

Hosley, Richard. "Was There a Dramatic Epilogue to *The Taming of the Shrew?" Studies in English Literature*, I (1961).

Houk, Raymond. "Shakespeare's Heroic Shrew," *Shakespeare Association Bulletin,* XVIII (1942).

Kuhl, Ernest P. "The Authorship of *The Taming of the Shrew*," *PMLA*, XL (1925).

Leggatt, Alexander. *Shakespeare's Comedy of Love.* London: Methuen, 1974.

Martz, William J. *Shakespeare's Universe of Comedy.* New York: David Lewis, 1971.

Parrott, Thomas M. *Shakespearean Comedy.* New York: Russell & Russell, Inc. 1962.

Pettet, E. C. *Shakespeare and the Romance Tradition.* London: Staples Press, 1949.

Prior, Moody E. "Imagery as a Test of Authorship," *Shakespeare Quarterly,* X (1955).

Richmond, Hugh M. *Shakespeare's Sexual Comedy: A Mirror for Lovers.* Indianapolis: Bobbs-Merrill Company, Inc. 1971.

Sanders, Norman. "Themes and Imagery in *The Taming of the Shrew*," *Renaissance Papers 1963*. Durham: North Carolina, 1964.

Sykes, H. Dugdale. *The Authorship of The Taming of the Shrew*. London: Chatto and Windus, 1919.

Tillyard, E. M. W. *Shakespeare's Early Comedies*. New York: Barnes & Noble, Inc., 1965.

Traversi, Derek. *Shakespeare: The Early Comedies*. London: Longman's, Green & Co., 1964.

Van Dam, B. A. P. *"The Taming of the Shrew,"* English Studies, X (1928).

Van Doren, Mark. *Shakespeare*. New York: Henry Holt, 1939.

Wilson, J. Dover. *Shakespeare's Happy Comedies*. London: Faber and Faber, 1962.